UNVERSED IN ARMS

UNVERSED IN ARMS

A SUBALTERN ON THE WESTERN FRONT

THE FIRST WORLD WAR DIARY
OF P. D. RAVENSCROFT MC
EDITED BY ANTONY BIRD

The Crowood Press

First published in 1990 by
The Crowood Press Ltd
Gipsy Lane, Swindon,
Wiltshire SN2 6DQ

This impression 1991

British Library Cataloguing in Publication Data
Ravenscroft, P.D.
Unversed in arms : the First World War diary of
P.D. Ravenscroft.
1. World War 1. Army operations by Great
Britain. Army – Biographies
I. Title   II. Bird, Antony
940.48141

ISBN 1-85223-539-X

Acknowledgements
The photographs appearing on pages 42, 66 and
154 are courtesy of the Royal Green Jackets
Museum, Winchester

Typeset by Chippendale Type Limited,
Otley, West Yorkshire.
Printed in Great Britain by
Billing & Sons Ltd, Worcester.

Contents

Acknowledgements

My thanks are due to Col. Ian McCausland (Retd) of the Royal Green Jackets for his kindness in making the diary available for publication. Thanks are also due to Ivor Snook and Jim Moriarty of the Royal Green Jackets Museum for their assistance.

The late PD Ravenscroft's son, Pelham Ravenscroft of Selbourne in Hampshire, has been most kind in answering enquiries about his father.

AEAB
1989

'All that a man might ask thou hast given me, England,
Yet grant thou one thing more:
That now when envious foes would spoil they splendour,
Unversed in arms, a dreamer such as I,
May in thy ranks be deemed not all unworthy,
England, for thee to die.'

RE Vernède, 2nd Lt. 3rd Battn Rifle Brigade, killed
May 8th 1917 aged 42.

Introduction

In November 1915 Pelham Donovan Ravenscroft, aged 24, late of Harrow School and Jesus College Cambridge, went to France as a 2nd Lt. with the Kings Royal Rifle Corps (60th Rifles) and was posted to the 2nd (Regular) Battalion, in which he served throughout the rest of the Great War, being promoted Captain only at its very end. In fact, by November 1918, he had become one of the longest serving officers in the Battalion, only one officer having the distinction of serving in the Battalion throughout the whole of the war. Ravenscroft had volunteered early in 1915, originally signing up with the Public Schools Battalion (16th Middlesex).

From his first day in France until more than three years later when he was demobbed, he kept a daily diary which he wrote on scraps of paper, later transcribing them into hard-bound volumes, with some added editorial notes in square brackets. It is this diary which is published here in its entirety, very few alterations having been made to the text.

Ravenscroft was born into a well-to-do family. However, while he was at Cambridge the family business, the Birkbeck Bank, failed and his family moved to a modest house at Chorleywood in Hertfordshire. On coming down from Cambridge, Ravenscroft took articles in London to train as an accountant, a career he resumed after the war. He had had a distinguished career at Cambridge, where he became President of the Footlights. He was to find ample scope for his musical and theatrical talents in the 2nd Battalion KRRC.

The 2nd Battalion KRRC (60th Rifles) was one of the six regular battalions of the Corps, serving with the 1st Division on the Western Front throughout the war and indeed in Germany after the Armistice. 'Corps' is in fact a bit of a misnomer. Although 23 new battalions were formed during the war it never fought as a single corps; its battalions were spread between 16 divisions. The 60th Rifles were so-called because they ranked 60th in the line. Originally called the 60th Royal Americans, the regiment was raised in 1755 to counter the marksmanship of the French-Canadian backwoodsmen of North America and until the 1840s it was composed mainly of foreign, and chiefly German, mercenaries (Arthur Bryant, *Jackets of Green*, Collins 1972). Their sister regiment, the Rifle Brigade (raised 1800),

7

Pelham Donovan Ravenscroft (1916).
[By permission of Pelham Ravenscroft Jnr].

is also somewhat confusingly named. It is a Regiment rather than a Brigade.

For most of his time with the Battalion, Ravenscroft served as a Lewis Gun Officer. He was awarded the MC at the end of the war, and was slightly wounded in September 1918, although seriously enough to become a statistic in the Battalion records. In the German Army such wounds did not get recorded.

Because the Battalion served from the earliest days of the war as a front line unit, casualties, particularly among officers, were shockingly high. The equivalent of its entire complement of 30 officers had been killed by the end of 1914, and between January 1915 and November 1918 another 90 officers were killed. No wonder Ravenscroft wrote on October 1st 1916 after the Somme Battles of High Wood and Mametz Wood that he was 'musing and marvelling at my being over the ground instead of under'.

The normal pattern of warfare for infantry battalions on the Western Front when not 'at rest' behind the lines was that roughly one third of the time would be spent in the front-line trenches, one third in reserve trenches and one third in billets behind the lines, often still within shell-fire of the enemy. Quite apart from fighting, the work of a battalion in the line was unceasing: repairing trenches, carrying stores, ammunition, rations, and of course wiring, usually carried out at night. It is worth pointing out that many of the tasks that officers such as Ravenscroft were required to perform were carried out in the German Army by NCOs. As a 2nd Lt., Ravenscroft's pay was seven shillings and sixpence per day.

Ravenscroft served in all the main sections of the Western Front, being at one time in 1917 the soldier on the extreme left or western end of the line at Nieuport Bains. It was here that he was unfortunate enough in this normally quiet sector to have been on the receiving end of a large German attack in which several of his fellow officers were captured, including 'Strafer' Gott. Although his baptism of fire came within ten days of arriving in France in the Loos sector, he was in no doubt that the worst experience he ever had was at High Wood on the Somme, where the carnage was worse than at Ypres in 1917.

And yet, of course, there were quiet times on the Western Front. There was swimming in the sea at Nieuport, there was a girl with 'pearl-white teeth and very neat feet' who cut Ravenscroft's hair, there were the concert parties, there were endless games of football and rugger; in fact the British Army, and riflemen in particular, seemed to have an all-consuming passion for sport, a trait attested to by Sir Arthur Bryant, himself a veteran of the war, in his history of the Rifle Brigade.

The Battalion attack on June 30th 1916, in which Ravenscroft participated, is interesting from the tactical point of view in that it nicely illustrates and epitomises all the difficulties experienced by attacking troops faced with a forewarned enemy, well dug-in, with wire and machine guns as well as artillery in place. The Battalion record is as follows and is worth quoting in full:

' . . . The battalion had parties selected for the attack . . . and by 8.30 p.m. were all ready. The zero hour was fixed at 9.10 p.m. At 9.00 p.m. the bridges [i.e. trench ladders] were put up. The enemy either saw them or the troops assembling in the trenches. At 9.03 p.m. they opened a heavy fire with trench mortar and artillery on our trenches causing many casualties as the trenches were crowded. Our artillery opened as arranged at 9.10 p.m. At 9.15 p.m. three mines were sprung and at 9.16 p.m. the storming parties went over the parapet. The two parties on the right failed to penetrate the heavy fire in front of the hostile trenches, and consequently what remained of them turned south, up the side of the north end of the Double Crassier in an attempt to help the Royal Sussex Regiment who had a company engaged there. These efforts to carry the German sap in the N Crassier together with the Royal Sussex did not succeed owing to wire and machine-gun fire. The centre column reached and entered the enemy's trench but found its right in the air and exposed to bombing attacks, nor did it succeed in joining up with the left column. Under the circumstances, Major WD Barber, the Senior Officer on the spot, ordered a withdrawal. This was carried out in good order. The losses were heavy: 11 officers of which 3 were killed, 2 died of wounds, 6 wounded. 28 ORs killed, 8 died of wounds, 24 missing, 167 wounded. The battalion accounted for some 100 enemy it is thought.'

Ravenscroft had been with Major Barber's centre column, being one of the five officers not killed or wounded. It was battles such as these that obsessed a whole generation and convinced military thinkers between the wars that some way must be found to prevent a repetition of this form of warfare.

But this diary is not primarily to be read from the point of view of infantry tactics. It is a dispassionate and yet moving account of one man's war, an account which articulates Capt. JC Dunn's dictum (Preface, *The War the Infantry Knew*, 1938) that 'a picture of the war from the front line standpoint, made without afterthought, will neither tickle a taste for foulness nor slake a thirst for pomp if it is drawn from what was seen and felt, and noted, at the time.'

PD Ravenscroft, who died in 1975, married 'Biddy' Gale in 1928, by whom he had two sons and one daughter.

Antony Bird
Chichester
1989

I

November 18th 1915 to December 31st 1916

1915

November

Thursday 18th
Left Charing Cross at 3 p.m. with Dunkels, OP Waller, FP Waller, Eminson and Edowes. We were all turned out at Folkestone Central with baggage. Raining and dark. Took a cab to the Harbour. Interviewed AMLO[1] who said we should not be crossing tonight. Secured rooms at the Royal Pavilion Hotel. Went to the theatre *Don't Tempt Me*, with the two Wallers and Eminson.

Friday 19th
Left Folkestone at 10.30 a.m. on the SS *Onward*. Lunched at the Hotel Meurice, Boulogne. Met Hugh Robinson[2] who was stationed in the best suite of the hotel. Wandered round the ramparts and went into the Cathedral. Dined at the Meurice and got into a very crowded train which landed us all at Etaples at 10.30 p.m. Very cold and full moon. Was given a couple of blankets and all six of us slept in a bell tent.

Saturday 20th
Washed and shaved in liquid ice and a draught. Breakfast at Lady Angela Forbes' Hut. Reported to OC Reinforcements. Attended lecture on 'Relieving Trenches' at 3.00 p.m. Took our other meals in the town.

Sunday 21st
Walked to Paris Plage and Le Touquet. Had lunch and visited a cinema. Dunkels acting as courier.

Monday 22nd
Paraded 8.45 a.m. About 400 of us, and marched to the training ground past several hospitals. Listened to a lecture on 'Bombing'.

The whole 400 were dismissed in the town at 12.30 p.m. and told to get our own lunch and attend another lecture in Camp at 3 p.m. on 'Feet, care of'. Took part in the scramble for lunch.

Tuesday 23rd
Paraded 8.45 a.m. as before. Revolver ammunition issued at 3 p.m. At 9.30 p.m. we six received orders to go up the line. Eminson, the two Wallers and myself to go to the 2nd Battn. Dunkels and Edowes to go to the 1st Battn.

Wednesday 24th
Got up at 1.45 a.m. and went to the Rly Siding about half a mile away. Sat on our baggage in the sand and dark till the train arrived at 5.30 a.m. Made my first meal of bully with a jack knife. Arrived at Béthune about 10 a.m. Walked behind GS[3] Wagon to Noeux-les-Mines, lunched there and rode on a limber at 3.30 p.m. to Mazingarbe. Saw Bosch 'archies' firing at our planes. Arrived at Mazingarbe in the dark, very muddy streets. Found our way to QM's[4] billet where we were greeted by 'Rob'. Ate large quantities of pork pie. Shared a bedroom with OP Waller.

Thursday 25th
Looked round in the morning. Met Roy Bullen[5] (Cambridge) who said he would get me posted to his Company (A).

Friday 26th
Waited for the Battn to come out of the line: they arrived at 1.30 a.m. (Saturday). Introduced to the Colonel (Bircham)[6]. Changed my billet to the school. Shared room with Archie Syminton and Shiney Holmes[7].

Saturday 27th
Feet inspection. Given No. 4 Platoon. Posted to A Coy.

Sunday 28th
Orderly Officer. Only duty was to visit guards.

Monday 29th
Rifle exercises in the rain. Kit inspection. Baths in vats at the Brewery.

Tuesday 30th
Sweeping and cleaning roads which needed it. Met 'Pocket' Dilius. Tea in Noeux-les-Mines.

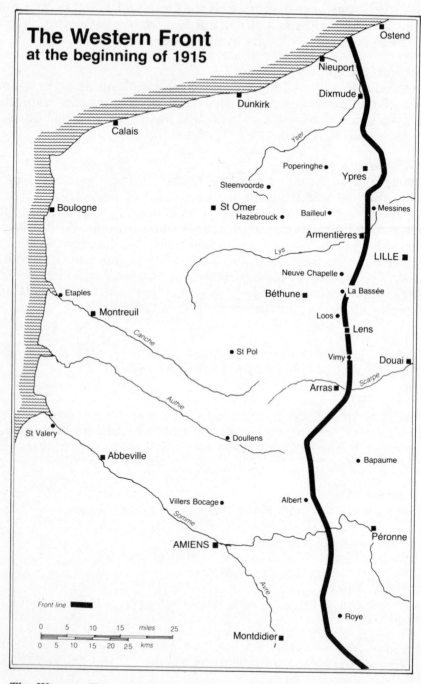

The Western Front
at the beginning of 1915

Ostend

Nieuport

Dixmude

Dunkirk

Yser

Calais

Poperinghe • Ypres

Steenvoorde •

Boulogne St Omer Bailleul • • Messines

Hazebrouck •

Armentières

Lys

LILLE

Neuve Chapelle •

Béthune La Bassée

• Etaples

Montreuil Loos •

Canche Lens

• St Pol Vimy • Douai

Authie Arras *Scarpe*

St Valery • Doullens

Abbeville • Bapaume

Villers Bocage • Albert

Somme

AMIENS Péronne

Avre

Front line

0   5   10   15 *miles* 25 • Roye

0 5 10 15 20 25 *kms* Montdidier

The Western Front at the beginning of 1915.

December

Wednesday 1st
Received my Baptism of Bosch 4.2″. One landed on the house opposite. A and D Coys messed together and I was somewhat surprised by the method of procedure adopted by our landlady with regard to the requirements of nature of her son aged about 4. It necessitated our praying for rain upon the doorstep. Went to Béthune, lorry jumping with OP in the afternoon. Bought a rubber bath which afterwards proved of inestimable value.

Thursday 2nd
Moved to Philosophe, a ruined village about 3km nearer the line. We were thus Battn in Reserve, our Brigade (the 2nd), holding the line. Saw a large fleet of our planes going East.

Friday 3rd
Received my canvas bucket (filled with chocolate biscuits) from Aunt Amy. Rain.

Saturday 4th
Battn went up into Support area. A Coy in '10th Avenue', part of the old German front line before Sept. 25th 1915 (Battle of Loos). Very muddy. Lost my revolver and case. Much discomfort.

Sunday 5th
Found my revolver in the mud and also a Bosch helmet badge slightly soiled. Accompanied a night digging party. Rain in the evening. High explosive shrapnel overhead.

Monday 6th
Rain in the evening. Dinkie Fryer arrived at A Coy from England (Sheerness).

Tuesday 7th
Took A Coy to continue digging the new trench. Rain in the evening.

Wednesday 8th
Battn took over front line. A Coy in close support by the junction of 'Posen Alley' with the Loos–Benefontanil Road. More discomfort. Mud over knees in the trenches and rusty rain dripping through the roof of the shelters.

Thursday 9th
HE shrapnel during lunch. Rain. Made my first visit to the front line. [I marvelled in the later years of the war at the way we all used to walk about unaccompanied without even telling anyone where we were going.]

Friday 10th
Big strafe by the Bosch at noon and at 3.30 p.m. Only 5 casualties. Rain.

Saturday 11th
Strafe during lunch. [It was most inconsiderate of the enemy to insist on this time of the day. We – that is Waller (OC), Symington, Holmes and myself – used to take up our positions sitting on SAA[8] boxes, each man in a separate traverse, balancing a tin plate, containing a veal cutlet and tinned peas with a flavour of sand and chalk, on our trembling knees. We didn't like the idea of staying in our one-entranced shelter which would keep out nothing but a shell splinter – not even rain.]

Our guns retaliated and set a Bosch dump alight. A very soothing sight seeing Bosch ammunition burning at a safe distance. When all was quiet I was appointed OC Pumps, i.e. I superintended the pumping of the trenches. [I put the end of the pipe on the side of the trench furthest from the Bosch so that they would not be able to see the water pouring out. Unfortunately the side I chose was lower than the country just beyond: the result was that about 75% of the water returned in miniature cascades to where it had just been expelled. As 100% of the water I expelled would have made no appreciable difference to the trench, it did not seem to be of much consequence if 75% returned.]

In the evening Archie spotted some partridges about 20 yards from the trench. He took careful aim with a rifle [Lewis guns had not yet been introduced] and winged two. He crawled out after them through mire and mud, but both managed to hop away. In the evening I accompanied the ration party to fetch rations from Gun Alley, the nearest point to which the limbers could approach.

Sunday 12th
Long strafe in the afternoon. Relieved by the 2nd Battn Royal Sussex Regt (in our Brigade). Marched through Loos and Fort Glatz to Philosophe to our same billets. Had a bath in the rubber one while supper was being laid. Although the soap got mixed with the butter, that bath was the finest I have ever had.

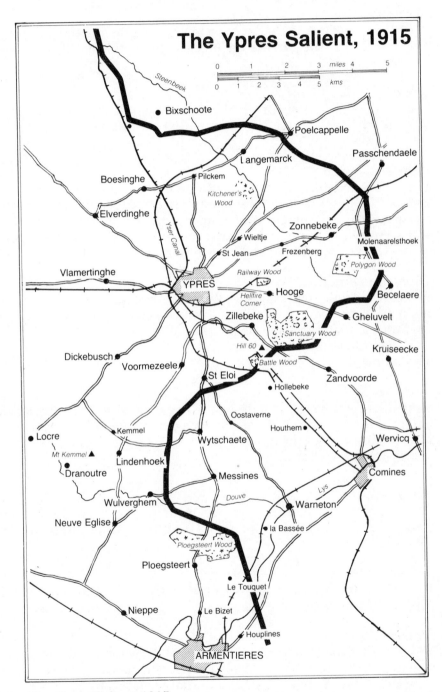

The Ypres Salient, 1915

The Ypres Salient 1915.

Monday 13th
The Slag Heap had 69 shells in the middle of it during the morning. Not one fell in the streets on houses. An artillery officer came in after tea.

Tuesday 14th
Visited Vervelles after lunch. Moved to Noeux-les-Mines 3.30 p.m. Messed with A, B and HQ in the Rue des Roses. Piano. Slept with Dinkie.

Wednesday 15th
Met Padre Kittermaster and discovered he was a master at Harrow[9]. Oppy (2nd in Command) invited Mademoiselle of the house to play the piano after dinner. She was too polite to stop and we were too polite to ask her to do so. However, she eventually completed her repertoire and therefore had to.

Thursday 16th
Went to Béthune with Dinkie. We each bought an ocarina; after the man in the shop had played the valse from the Pink Lady on one, we couldn't very well help it. Met Edowes.
   Wallington (Adjt. of the Sussex) came to dinner. Much piano and ocarina playing.

Friday 17th
Rehearsal for concert at 2.30 p.m. Concert at 5 p.m. in the large hall behind the church. There was a stage with scenery and curtain. Most successful. All the officers of the Battn dined in our mess. Rag and music afterwards.

Saturday 18th
CO talked to us about a raid we were to make on the Bosch. Called for volunteers but as we all volunteered he ended up by selecting 2 or 3.

Sunday 19th
Bright sunny day. Pitched 164 tents at Houchin in the morning. Met Chad who was doing the same with his party of Sussex.

Monday 20th
Battn took over Front Line. I joined B Coy temporarily in the absence of Cull and Savin. Went up via Mazingarbe, Vervelles, le Routoire Alley, Wings Way B2. Palatial shelter and fairly strong. Only one entrance.

Tuesday 21st
Quiet. Rain.

Wednesday 22nd
Rain. Visited Fison's dug-out and trench mortar. Saw a hand sticking out of the side of a trench.

Thursday 23rd
Fine morning. Visited a lot of saps with names of Welsh towns. Got a small Bosch bomb (cricket ball type).

Friday 24th
Big strafe in the early morning. Mine blown on our left. Trench fell in owing to the wet in a dozen places. Relieved by 1st Northants. Went back to Philosophe. A different billet in the main Lens–Béthune Road. Rejoined A Coy.

Saturday 25th
Small concert at 5 p.m. I accompanied the comic songs on a weak-kneed harmonium. The Brigadier was present (Brig.-Gen. Twillor). Rowdy evening in Mess, which was next to HQ Mess, with crackers and musical instruments. The Colonel thought it was the HQ Signals making the noise, so sent out to put them under arrest. All was well, however.

Sunday 26th
Half Battn went back into support. A Coy in a different part of '10th Avenue'. North of Posen Station. Walley[10] and I were the only A Coy officers. Symington was left out practising for the 'folly' (the Raid). Our dug-out was wallpapered in places and full of rats.

Monday 27th
Carried coils of barbed wire for the Sussex. The mud was awful, well over the knees and of the sticky variety. Very dark night. Essex Lane was the worst part, in fact part of it was abandoned afterwards and a new piece dug. Several men left their boots in the mud and of course several more dumped their loads. We started as soon as it was dark and I got back to my rats at 1 a.m. Wrapped myself in my blanket and drank two large mugs of port. Slept well and undisturbed by the vermin.

Tuesday 28th
Helped RE revet[11] the front line in the afternoon. Went to see Col. Villiers (Sussex) about the wire, and had the same job in the evening again. Mud worse, if possible. Shiney Holmes joined us.

19

Wednesday 29th
Fine day and a slack one.

Thursday 30th
Took over front line BI via Essex Lane. Terrific strafe just as we started. Mine blown on our left. Went out on patrol to find a supposed Bosch listening post in an old gun pit. Took 3 so-called bombers with me [Mills bombs were new then]. After I'd been out wandering about on my knees in the mud for some time, the bombers informed me that they couldn't pull out the pins. I thought that a discreet moment for retiring and writing my report. The General Staff were satisfied that no listening post was used in that sector by the enemy.

Friday 31st
An officer and platoon of the Irish Rifles arrived to be attached to us for instruction (the 16th Division). I was struck by the excellence of their NCOs. Quiet day. Small Bosch strafe at 11 p.m., the German midnight, to usher in the New Year[12].

1916

January

Saturday 1st
Relieved by 1st Black Watch (1st Bde). Marched to Philosophe where we embussed in LGO[13] Coy's buses[14] painted service green. I sat on the top step of the staircase, a most excellent position on rough roads. Arrived Noeux-les-Mines about 9 p.m. Had a good supper at HQ Mess. My billet was quite comfortable but lacked carpet and furniture except a large double bed.

Sunday 2nd
Bottle of Grand Marnier arrived from home. A Coy's mess was in a butcher's shop at the Monument. We had another Christmas dinner and danced to the gramophone afterwards. I walked into the back yard to get a little fresh air and unfortunately walked into a very deep cesspool. My head did not go under, but I failed to touch the bottom. My return to the ballroom caused considerable mirth, even amongst the two female civilians who had been watching the dance from a conservatory. We did not ask them to join in. I thought it time to retire and discard my somewhat soiled garments. We had all taken off our tunics long before so that and the contents of its

pockets were saved. The bareness of my room now proved most useful. I laid out my clothes, after wringing them out of the window, on the floor. Next day my excellent servant, Read, dealt with them and I wore them for many a month afterwards.

Monday 3rd

A third Christmas dinner at HQ Mess; all officers attended. A turkey formed the chief attraction. Walley *would* sing 'They wouldn't believe me' from *Tonight's the Night* afterwards. [He had also sung this at our little concert at Philosophe, but my harmonium accompaniment had been too much for him and words failed. I happened to remember them so we finished as a duet.]

Tuesday 4th

Rose at 6 a.m. to take a working party to Fosse No.1 at Bracquement which was [then] in the French area. After hunting about for an hour found the RE[15] officer in charge. Our work consisted of removing the red slag for road-making. Listened to the 1st Div. Band 5–7 p.m.

Wednesday 5th

Took A Coy for a route march round by Houchin. Lovely day and thoroughly enjoyed it. Played overture for Northants concert at 5 p.m. Kittermaster came to dinner.

Thursday 6th

Another route march through Sailly-Labourse. Orderly officer.

Friday 7th

Took over front line at Chalk Pit Wood. Deep dug-out with two entrances. 2 officers and a platoon of Royal Dublin Fusiliers attached to us.

Saturday 8th

My platoon sergeant, Sgt. Bentley went sick with a sprained ankle.

Sunday 9th

'The Jolly Boy's Show', i.e. the Raid on the Bosch. [Archie had been trying to cut wire during the past week. Our guns strafed at 10 p.m. and midnight. At the latter hour our people went over with black faces and their swords[16] draped in crepe. There was a further row of wire that had not been cut. However, there were no Bosch there, so we came back. I watched proceedings

21

with the CO and Dunkels from the front line.] We only had 3 casualties.

Monday 10th
Not much retaliation on the whole. A fine day. Dinkie went out in the evening to bring back telephones left out by our people the night before.

Tuesday 11th
Relieved by Sussex. Went to the Reserve line which I had dug in the beginning of December. Quite clean, no rats and the Bosch didn't know it was occupied. Short strafe on our left just before we left front line.

Wednesday 12th
Fine day. Gun Alley strafed behind us.

Thursday 13th
Laid trench-boards in new CT[17] from Strand Alley to Loos Alley. Brady and Cull visited us. Had a most amusing discussion on women and marriage with Walley and Dinkie.

Friday 14th
Relieved late by a battn of Camerons of the 15th Division. Buses from Philosophe to Noeux as before. Same billet.

Saturday 15th
Divisional relief. Entrained at Noeux for Lillers. Lunch at the Hotel du Commerce opposite the station. After lunch we went to see Archie's friends at the corner café. [The Battn had rested at Lillers before so all the old stagers had friends in the town. The names of two of these particular three were Germaine and Margot. Their speciality was strawberry champagne – a gaseous fluid, pale pink in colour.]

Sunday 16th
Church Parade in the Theatre, 11 a.m. Padre Blackburne 1st Div. Padre officiated. Archie received the MC. Went to ASC[18] officers' concert. Good.

Monday 17th
Started on a Wiring Course under Div. RE's. Went to see Nell, one of the ASC officers, to get him to sing at our forthcoming concert.

Tuesday 18th
Tea with Fison who was helping with the concert. Ran through some songs.

Wednesday 19th
Went to an RAMC[19] pantomime. Very good. Ordered skull caps and other props for my concert.

Thursday 20th
Joffre[20] inspected the 1st Div. I got out of it by attending my wiring course. He was very late. Had my hair cut by a very pleasant girl with pearl-like teeth and very neat feet. Rehearsal in D Coy's Mess.

Friday 21st
Rehearsal in the theatre with the 1st Div. Band. Went to Burbure Range with the Coy in the morning. Had my photo taken.

Saturday 22nd
Rode Prince to the Range before breakfast. Walked out again after. Set the scene and rehearsed in the afternoon. Concert at 7 p.m. I played the cornet. First appearance of A Coy officers' pierrot troupe. Roy Bullen sang 'China Town'. Chorus with tin hats [then a novelty] to give a Chinese effect. [This concert was a great success, the old regular officers being quite pleased. Had a great struggle to overcome various criticisms and suggestions by the aforesaid, whose minds were military rather than artistic. A senior officer's suggestion sounds so like a command.]

Sunday 23rd
Orderly officer. Not very well. Indigestion and chill caught by getting hot at the theatre and remaining in a draught.

Monday 24th
Went out with the Coy to the two windmills at Hurionville in the morning. Football in the afternoon, but didn't play.

Tuesday 25th
Went to Lespesses in the morning with the Coy. Paid out in the afternoon. Received my photos.

Wednesday 26th
Went to Hurionville and Burbane. Men had baths. Shiney Holmes slightly wounded by a premature Mills bomb. He went to the CCS[21] in the town.

Thursday 27th
Range 8.30–1.30 p.m. Brigade put on 2 hours' notice to move owing to rumours of a Bosch attack. [This was the beginning of Verdun [22]].

Friday 28th
Battn went to the Woods SE of Allouagne for wood fighting practice. Had a bath at the 'Fumé' Co-op Stores. Went to a concert at 7.30 p.m. Kemsley Rutherford sang and CF Smiley accompanied him. Talked to Smiley afterwards; he was in the Artists Rifles and a Sgt. instructor of Vickers MG at Wisques.

Saturday 29th
Took the Company to the Range at 8.15 a.m. Called back by orderly as Brigade was on 2 hours' notice again. Boxing in the theatre 5 p.m.

Sunday 30th
Brigade open air service 10.30 a.m.

Monday 31st
Still on 2 hours' notice. Coy Drill etc. Soccer – best platoon of A Coy v C Coy. A won. [Walley who was at the time OC A Coy, had borrowed a pair of large tailor's scissors from a shop in order to experiment with GS overcoats so that they would not collect the mud so easily. He informed me of the charm of the owners of the scissors, so I went with him to return them. He was right, and they regaled us with excellent coffee.] He went on leave that night and left me temporarily OC.

February

Tuesday 1st
Took my first Coy office. Paid out. A v D at soccer. Result a draw. Played rugger for the Battn against the Rhodesians of the Battn. We lost 14–5 (B Coy had a platoon of Rhodesians and 2 or 3 officers. They had and maintained a high reputation and were very 'stout fellows').

Wednesday 2nd
Bde back to 6 hours' notice. Battn attacked the Hurionville windmills. Archie in command of A Coy. I, with magnificent bravery, led a platoon round the flanks of the enemy (if windmills have flanks) and captured the position. At that moment Oppy galloped

up in a most excitable state and told me I had been wiped out with my whole platoon long ago. [I seemed fated, during my training both in England and France, to attack windmills, so much so that my Christian namesake Quixote[23] was continually in my mind during these adventures.] Night operations during which I twisted my ankle.

Thursday 3rd
Dinkie returned from a bombing course at Ferfay. Took orderly officer as ankle was swollen. Got Coy money from Field Cashier. Watched Div. boxing in the afternoon. Mess meeting to consider better method of apportioning mess bills.

Friday 4th
Rain caused Battn operations to be cancelled. Short route march. Tea with Readdie at the Oyster Shop. Listened to band in theatre and accompanied Archie and Padre Blackburne on piano.

Saturday 5th
Bde march and operations at Ecquidiques. Lunch in a stubble field at 4 p.m.

Sunday 6th
Church parade in theatre 10 a.m. News of cancellation of a great trek received at dinner. Much relief.

Monday 7th
Div. route march Ecquidiques, Lières, Auchez au Bois, St Hilliare, Lillers. Auchez au Bois was quite deserted. Grass and moss all over the street and houses. Great cracks in most of the houses. [I believe a big coal mine explosion had been the cause many years ago, and the villagers, who were chiefly miners, built a new village nearby.] Archie and I tried to get our leave warrants so that we could get an extra day by starting a day early. We went to Bde and they sent us to Div. Archie had got them from a junior staff officer and was just leaving the room when the AA & QMG[24] came in. He said he had given too many people their warrants early and we must either wait till tomorrow or come back a day early. Archie decided to have them now and return early. I waited outside during this, as we thought it tactful for only one to approach these great men, and a 1st Lt. with a brand new MC would be more suitable than I.

Tuesday 8th
As our train didn't leave till 3 a.m. we prevented ourselves from

going to sleep by playing every record, good or bad, on the gramophone. I don't know whether other people were similarly prevented from sleeping. Got a first class carriage and arrived Boulogne 10 a.m. and breakfasted at the Louvre. Left on SS *Victoria* at 12.15 p.m. Arrived Folkestone 2.20 p.m. The sensation of sitting in a smooth fast-moving Pullman on one's first leave and seeing English country and advertisements – even advertisements – flying by, is very good. I never felt it on my successive leaves. Arrived Victoria 5.15 p.m. Went to Hippodrome *Joyland*.

First Leave

February

Tuesday 15th
Left Victoria 9.15 a.m. Lunch at Royal Pavilion Hotel Folkestone. Collared for duty at Victoria but only meant hanging about at Folkestone which I should have done in any case. Crossed to Boulogne on SS *Onward* at 4.30 p.m. Met Hugh Robinson at the Meurice and slept there. Dined at the Commerce – an amusing place.

Wednesday 16th
Breakfast at Meurice, left for Béthune at 1.25 p.m. Arrived about 7 p.m. Slept at Station Hotel.

Thursday 17th
Train to Noeux arrived 12 noon. Spotted by Regt. QMS Crabtree who put me on a GS wagon with the rations for Les Brebis. Lunch with Rob. Tea with Dinkie who was now a Bde Bomber and lived with the Bde Trench Mortar officer. Wakely was also there. Reported to Battn HQ at the Loos end of Maroc at 7 p.m. Dinner with A Coy in support trench by Middle Alley near the Double Crassier[25].

Friday 18th
Cleaned and pumped Middle Alley and the Embankment. Battn relieved that night and went to the Garden City Maroc. Carried stores for RE to the D. Crassier. RE guide lost his way and took us through all the mud he could find. Told to do a second journey but so fed up I rang up the Adjt., Philip Currie, who agreed that 2nd journey was too much. Slept on a lean spring mattress in cellar of quite a good house. Only a miner's villa but it had 4 more or less complete walls.

Saturday 19th
Breakfast 11 a.m. Visited St James' Keep, a strong point in village line, with Shiney in the evening. Beautiful night with full moon. Heard aeroplane with MG [a novelty to us in those days].

Sunday 20th
'Gas Alert' in morning[26]. Relieved by Northants at 9 p.m. They were late as they had lost their way. Arrived Bracquement 11 p.m.

Monday 21st
Stood to at a moment's notice as Bosch were attacking the French on our right. Intense bombardment all day, but our village was left alone. Put on half hour's notice at 10 p.m. Slept in clothes – a pity as the bed was very comfortable. (Perhaps it was as well as the old lady of the house had to pass through my room to get to hers).

Tuesday 22nd
Took party for RE work on new rear line near Mazingarbe. Met the Royal Scots (15th Div.) who had relieved us (1st Div.) in January. Snowstorm. Roy turned up in the evening from Div. where he was on the learner's course, vulgarly known as 'Dobby's Lambs'. Dobby was GSOI[27].

Wednesday 23rd
Took party to Fosse No. 2 for baths. Good baths at the Pit Head. [They were divided by low partitions and the boilers and taps etc. were built high up. Girls controlled the taps and gauges from the top of a flight of steps. It seemed odd, but they were used to it.] More snow. Tea at the Globe in Noeux. This was being started as an officers' tea room. A pasty-faced damsel with golden hair attended to our wants.

Thursday 24th
Heard of Bosch 30 mile attack down south (Verdun). Coy Commanders visited front line. Tea at Globe again with Waller and Shiney. Had a liqueur at the Wine Shop which contained the village belle. People came even from Béthune to see her. Also pasty-faced.

Friday 25th
2nd Div. came through Bracquement to relieve the French on our right. Saw our 1st Battn pass by. More snow. Globe and Wine Shop again.

Saturday 26th
Took over front line between Loos and the Double Crassier via the Haymarket. Halted on the way at Les Brebis and had a hasty cup of tea with the Bde MG Coy. Thaw and more snow.

Sunday 27th
Had the 60lb TM explained to me. Fine morning. Thaw. McMillan (B Coy) hit. He died of wounds later. We blew mines on our left. Got wiring parties out.

Monday 28th
Took party of 8 men and 3 scouts out on an 'offensive patrol'. No offensiveness. Snow all gone.

Tuesday 29th
Glorious morning. Spring. Birds and shells whistling. Lots of aeroplanes up. Relieved by Northants. Went to D area Les Brebis.

March

Wednesday 1st
All A officers dined with D. Only Gibb and Dunlavey there as hosts. We played the piano but were requested to stop as a shell had dropped in the garden during the afternoon and Madame had a headache.

Thursday 2nd
Went by bus to Ferfay for Lewis Gun Course. Met Aubrey Dickenson[28] (2nd Battn) there. Played bridge with him and Sainton (Sussex) in a comfortable billet with fire and electric light. The school was 1st Div. and in an unfurnished château. Very draughty.

Friday 3rd
Snow in the afternoon. Hogged it in my warm billet after tea. No electric light in mine.

Saturday 4th
More snow. Aubrey left.

Sunday 5th
Fired in the morning. Walked to Lillers with Beale (8th Royal Berks) for lunch at the Commerce. Had my hair cut by my former artiste. Walked back in intermittent showers of sleet.

Monday 6th
Heavy snow and lying thick. Tea in Waller's mess. (He had come for a bombing course). Realised how fortunate we were not to be in the line. Sent my servant Read to get money from Lillers.

Tuesday 7th
Snowing.

Wednesday 8th
Snow on the ground. Glorious evening. Walked to Amettes and Ames. Hummed every tune in *Tonight's the Night* to relieve the solitude. Concert at 6 p.m.

Thursday 9th
Was examined by my instructor, a L/Cpl in the Motor MG Corps. Exam over by 10 a.m. Walked to Auchel and back to lunch. Snow still on the ground.

Friday 10th
Went to Lillers for lunch with Beale. Bought some books. Still snow on ground.

Saturday 11th
Returned in lorries to Les Brebis. Heard the Band play 'Bric à Brac' that I had got for them. Dunkels to dinner. Went round to Angel's mess (MG) after tea.

Sunday 12th
Church Parade 10.30 a.m. Played hymns on piano. Grammy Stafford (1st Battn) came to tea.

Monday 13th
Stokes arrived back from the base. Laughton joined, Doug White-hall in the evening. Got some cocoa from Trench Maintenance Sgt.

Tuesday 14th
Rode Kitty to Noeux and back. Listened to band. Stokes came to dinner. Spring day.

Wednesday 15th
Gas test in the morning. Took our front line via Edgeware Road. 2nd Div. on our right. Slight cold in the eyes.

Thursday 16th
Maj.-Gen. Holland (GOC 1st Div.) came in, to see about filling up
some of the old French trenches that we didn't use. Doc Ward
explained the Vermoral Sprayer[29]. Quiet day.

Friday 17th
Quiet day except for a few TMs. Examined Point 16 with glasses
in a sniper's post with Ashton (a sniper). No luck. Strange mist in
the evening – thought it was gas.

Saturday 18th
Explored Quarry Road and Maroc Fosse and took the Coy there in
the evening for digging. Evidently much wind up at HQ as Gunners
and ASC were wiring reserve lines in front of us with feverish
haste. Relieved by Northants. Went to Maroc Garden City.

Sunday 19th
Took those of A and B Coys who were not digging down to billets
in Petit Sains. Rode Jane. Supper in B Coy's mess.

Monday 20th
More digging in the R. Irish Fusiliers area. They had just gone into
the line for the first time as a Division (16th). My platoon Sgt.
unfortunately had consumed more rum than he could stand.

Tuesday 21st
Court of Enquiry on above Sgt. Went to Noeux for tea with Gibb
and Egerton-Green. Aubrey to dinner. Roy went on leave.

Wednesday 22nd
Went back to same billets in Maroc. Filled in trenches at night.
Shiney OC Coy.

Thursday 23rd
Cold day. Went for a stroll with Shiney after tea. A night off
fatigues at last.

Friday 24th
Elsie Barnes and Blackett arrived to A and D Coys respectively.
Took over front line via Neuf Alley. Snow and cold. CSM Buchanan
arrived back.

Saturday 25th
Cold but warm in the sun. Snow melted.

Sunday 26th
Rain p.m. Rifleman Richmond (LG) killed.

Monday 27th
Relieved by Black Watch. Returned to Les Brebis. I was bringing up the rear and noticed we were not going the right way. Pushed by half a Coy to find that it had lost the front half. Proceeded to lead them and arrived safely.

Tuesday 28th
Fatigue on the Rly during the day. Band were innoculated so couldn't play. Cigars arrived.

Wednesday 29th
Kit inspection in morning.

Thursday 30th
Rode to Noeux for Battn money. Archie splinter came down within a foot of us. The horse heard it first and jumped. Walley, who had gone to Ferfay for LG course came over to lunch. Fatigue at 6 p.m. on North Street, N of Loos Crossier.

Friday 31st
'Snodders' Maxwell arrived. Gibb went on leave so I asked if I could take on the LG sections while he was away. Box respirators (large) were looked at. Johnny Johnstone[30] showed us all about Rifle Grenades.

April

Saturday 1st
Rose at 5 a.m. Explored Loos. One of the LG team shot another. Not killed. Attended FGCM[31] in afternoon on my platoon Sgt. A area of the village (ours) was shelled. Saw aeroplane come down in flames for the first time. Aubrey to dinner.

Sunday 2nd
Took over Loos cellars. Fatigue in Regent Street which had been blown in badly in the afternoon.

Monday 3rd
Went round LG posts with Attwater (Northants). Bodies were being dug out of the quarry after yesterday's strafe. Told to find

a LG emplacement on Loos Crassier. Searched the whole of it. Wasn't one; wrote report saying so. Explored the remains of the Power Station and the Tower Bridge. For a wonder the Bosch did not strafe it while I was there. Very interesting. Saw boilers, gauges and winding gear in various stages of mutilation.

Tuesday 4th
Roy returned. Tea with Attwater in North Street.

Wednesday 5th
Took over front line via Seaforth Alley. Egerton-Green came to us temporarily from B Coy. While having dinner with Shiney in the shelter, the food suddenly jumped off the table. We looked at each other. 'Mine' said Shiney. We rushed out and found a crater which had just missed the front line but had caught a sap and buried two men. Oppy happened to be in our Coy area at the time. He decided that the crater was not worth occupying. Tremendous excitement, but not many casualties. I bespattered the crater which the Bosch had occupied with LG enfilade fire from the Crossier.

Thursday 6th
An awful calm. Nobody knew what the Bosch were going to do next. B Coy came up in close support. Northants in reserve. Some scheme for attacking the crater, but cancelled.
   Quiet rainy night.

Friday 7th
Shiney, who had been anxious about his leave during the last two days, bolted the moment we stood down in the morning. We all cheered up again. Big strafe at lunch time with TMs and 5.9″s.

Saturday 8th
Nothing much during the day. Sappers blew a camouflet[32] as we were on the way out being relieved. Of course the Bosch retaliated and caught us in the CTs. Luckily they were deep and narrow and we suffered no damage. Went to OGI (Old German front line) by Piccadilly. Very nice and quiet with good strong dug-outs.

Sunday 9th
Peaceful. Explored various old trenches.

Monday 10th
Quiet. Looked for the Bomb Store in Loos. Saw the Bosch 16-inch dud with a Pip Squeak[33] lying beside it. Called on D Coy in E

Way. Carried stores to front line. Everybody lost their way. Got back at 3 a.m.

Tuesday 11th
Took over cellars in Loos. Took over Northants LG and had tea with Attwater.

Wednesday 12th
Rain. Had notice that a proposed attack by us on the Triangle near the Double Crassier was put off. Not at all sorry as there was a solid mass of rusty barbed wire in front of it 50-yards deep all the way. The Bosch also held most of the Double Crassier which looked right down on to the Triangle. They also had mines under the North end of it.

Thursday 13th
Dunlavey wounded badly.

Friday 14th
While we were having lunch in our cellar there was a most appalling crash. We went out to see what had happened and saw the left tower of Loos collapsing. The Bosch were always trying to hit them. Relieved by Black Watch and returned to Les Brebis.

Saturday 15th
Listened to Band 5–7. Music with Blackett at Dinkie's and Readdie's house. Charming people. Very good piano, just delivered from Lille before the Bosch got there.

Sunday 16th
Church Parade. Lewis Gun Meeting at 2nd Bde MG HQ at Grennay. Pearson (Bubbly Jock) presided. Webb arrived to A Coy. Listened to Monsieur at D Coy's mess (whose landlady had a headache before) play cello.

Monday 17th
Saw Fricker (LGO Northants) re LG's Exhibition of Smoke Barrage on Bombing Ground 7 p.m. Rained at the end and I got very wet.

Tuesday 18th
Lecture by Col. MacNaughton RFA 6.30 p.m. Held competition of stripping and assembling LGs.

Wednesday 19th
Went round the line by the Double Crassier in the morning.

Thursday 20th
Took over the front line just opposite the Triangle from the 6th Welsh (3rd Bde). Slept in very small shelter with Aubrey, C Coy and Freeman, D Coy. Most disgusting trench after all our work. Rain had made Middle Alley knee-deep and exposed.

Friday 21st
Rain in torrents but quiet. Explored an old trench and nearly had to swim. Had to turn back. Dried my knees over a brazier. Saw Blackett after he'd been patrolling and he was one cake of mud with a liquid surface.

Saturday 22nd
Rain in more torrents. Trenches falling in at every traverse. Middle Alley a mere ditch and but for a mist would have been completely exposed. Freeman left to visit dentist at Béthune. Wise man.

Sunday 23rd
Fine day. Relieved by Sussex. Went to Garden City Maroc.

Monday 24th
Fine day. Some strafing in the early morning. Laid armoured telephone cable in Sickly Alley.

Tuesday 25th
Strafing in early morning. Our guns cut wire in the afternoon. Laid more cable.

Wednesday 26th
Took over front line from Sussex. Small mine blown by Bosch in B Coy's area. Moore who had just arrived and who was in command of B, much perturbed. The Sussex who had not gone took no notice of it. I had to alter LG positions and OP Waller stayed there all night with Rifle Grenades bouncing off his tin hat[34].

Thursday 27th
Bosch bombarded on our left (Chalk Pit Wood) with Smoke. Wind up and thought it was gas. Very intense while it lasted.

Friday 28th
Northants did a raid in the evening. We blew a large camouflet. Pretty good retaliation by Bosch.

Saturday 29th
Gas attack on our left (16th Div.) in the early morning. We got the gas slightly. A group of A Coy were standing at the mouth of a dug-out with the old PH[35] helmets on so couldn't hear a TM coming. The one TM killed Roy Bullen and 5 others and wounded 8. Relieved by Sussex and returned to Maroc. Roy and the others buried in Maroc Cemetery at 10 p.m.

Sunday 30th
Left Bde got wind up and sent SOS at 11 p.m. Cancelled soon after. Brady arrived back and took over A Coy. I slept with C Coy. Played cricket in the evening in the street with a house between us and the Bosch balloon.

May

Monday 1st
Moore took over A Coy and Brady took over B Coy. I slept again with C Coy. More cricket.

Tuesday 2nd
Bosch woke us up by strafing Fosse II. Relieved by 10th Gloucester (1st Bde). Went to Petit Sains. Rode Lady which became the LGO's horse. A very fast trotter, but apt to fall down. Wore puttees on at least 3 legs. Cricket in evening.

Wednesday 3rd
General (French?) (Kitchener?) distributed medals at Bracquement. Didn't go. Visited wine shop with Stokes. Listened to strafe after dinner.

Thursday 4th
Hair cut at Noeux. Rounders in the evening.

Friday 5th
Listened to Band at Bracquement with Snodders. Played rounders. Brady left and Moore went back to B.

Saturday 6th
LG Physical Drill. Rode with Aubrey to Bovigny, Sains en Gohelle

and district. Very pretty country. Looked into Lens from the top of Notre Dame de Lorette ridge. Played rounders in evening.

Sunday 7th
Went up to look round front line by Harrison's crater. Dinkie arrived from Bde bombing to take over A Coy. Shiney went to Bde bombers. Stokes went to Ferfay. Dinner with C Coy.

Monday 8th
Battn took over front line at Harrison's Crater from 6th Welsh (3rd Bde). Lived in South Street with A Coy and did a little company work as well.

Tuesday 9th
Rain. Elsie Barnes arrived back.

Wednesday 10th
Started building steel girder emplacements, neither I nor my L Gunners knowing anything about it.

Thursday 11th
Bosch strafed with 8". Buried over 20 men and one of my guns which was not damaged much. The team was isolated as the trench on each side of them was blown flat. I did a little mountaineering on my tummy amongst the white chalk in and out of craters and shell-holes, and eventually reached them. Relieved by Northants and went to N Maroc. Much strafing up North in the evening.

Friday 12th
Had to send up two teams under Bde orders to carry on the emplacements. I went up at night and came back to N Maroc to sleep during the day.

Saturday 13th
Went up again, had dinner with Readdie in Trench Mortar House, an excellent spot just outside Loos. Strolled into Loos in the evening and watched all the different rations parties and RE stores unloading. The *Place* by the Church was a mass of shouting individuals that reminded me of Covent Garden Market. One well-placed shell would have laid out scores of men, horses and limbers. All quiet except for an occasional bullet ricocheting off a wall.

Sunday 14th
Changed the gun teams. Battn went into front line again. Lived at Trench Mortar House with Readdie and Pearson (LGO Northants)

and rationed by D Coy. Bosch raided the Sussex on our left and collared a LG. Edwardes arrived.

Monday 15th
Irish LGO came round with some NCOs. Showed them all round the posts. Discussed with RE officer the emplacements and dug-outs that I was building, also discussed the possibility of an invention of an RE for Lewis Gun Mounting in emplacements. South Street altered, as a result of which I lost my way.

Tuesday 16th
We and the Bosch working hard in front of our lines strengthening wire etc. Very quiet on each side for each others' sakes. Handed LGs over to Dent.

Wednesday 17th
Showed Irish LGs into their places as they were taking over down to Loos inclusive and we were side-slipping to the right. Left Loos at 3 p.m. Bath and tea at Les Brebis. Rode to Béthune. Dinner at the Peon d'Or 8 p.m. Got into train at 11 p.m. Corner seat, 1st class.

Thursday 18th
Left Béthune 2.20 p.m., arrived Boulogne 10 a.m. Crossed on SS *Queen* at 11.30 a.m. Arrived Folkestone about 12.45 p.m. and Victoria 3.30 p.m. Just over 24 hours from leaving Loos unshaven and dirty. Went to *Bing Boys Are Here* at Alhambra.

Second Leave

Clocks put forward in England, Sunday 21st.

Friday 26th
Left Victoria 8.30 a.m. Spent day at Folkestone. Crossed on *Invicta* at 7.30 p.m. Met Vivian Grey and Bullen's brother (Scottish Rifles) at Folkestone. Met Dunkels. Collared for duty on the boat and marched men up to the Camp all up hill. When I got back again went to Meurice too late for dinner. Hot, tired and angry. Vowed I'd never do it again. Had bread and cheese and went to bed.

Saturday 27th
Fetched these men from their exalted camp at 11.30 a.m. Left Boulogne about 1 p.m. Arrived Béthune 7 p.m. Bus to Les Brebis.

Rob told me that Battn was at Petit Sains. Horse to P. Sains. Dinner at Battn HQ. Heard about the Revised Triangle show for the 1st June[36].

Sunday 28th
Watched rehearsal for the Show. The ground was all marked out representing the trenches. A haystack represented a mine crater we were to blow and a Rly embankment the Double Crassier. Listened to Band at Bracquement in afternoon with Shiney. Not at all well. Bad night.

Monday 29th
Saw the Doc. Temperature. Quiet all day.

Tuesday 30th
Fortunately announced that I was better before the CO announced that GHQ had put off the Show. Stayed another night at Petit Sains.

Wednesday 31st
Took over front line to left of Middle Alley from Northants. Stayed with A Coy. Got on with building.

June

Thursday 1st
Pip-squeaked during the day. LG who was digging a dug-out suddenly came across a dark chamber with cold air rushing out. Wind up and thought it was a Bosch mine gallery. Called in RE assistance. Everyone bewildered. Eventually found it was our other staircase round the traverse. I was quite pleased that they had met at all even though at different levels. Buried up to my waist while getting from one staircase to another, by a fall of the roof.

Friday 2nd
Got the 173rd Tunnelling Coy RE to look at the staircases, but they had nothing to suggest but start again in another place. Couldn't do that because Div. had selected the tactical position. Relieved the teams.

Sunday 4th
Battn relieved by Northants and went into Support. I lived with D Coy in OGI.

Monday 5th
Endeavoured to get supply of candles from Adjt. for dug-out building as buying them from the mess was becoming expensive.

Tuesday 6th
Coy Commanders and I went round Maroc defenses with the CO. Rained. Sladen arrived. Got the Lowland REs to look at the dug-outs. Relieved the teams again.

Wednesday 7th
Took Sladen exploring round about the Loos end of North Street. Kept on meeting generals and other red hats. This was in the Irish Div. (16th) area. Battn relieved Northants. I lived in new deep dug-out in Middle Alley with C Coy.

Thursday 8th
Explored a piece of OGI just reopened to traffic. Dent hit by our own sentry.

Friday 9th
C Coy short of officers so took trench patrols for them.

Saturday 10th
Relieved by 8th Berks. LG at 12.30 p.m. Battns relieved when dark. Met Shiney. Had dinner with Eminson, who was now in Bde MG Coy. Had heated argument with Bubbly Jock over 'Dug-out building'. Lived with A Coy. Thunderstorm.

Sunday 11th
Rain.

Monday 12th
Started preparing for concert with officers' pierrot troupe with Blackett. Ordered pom-poms from local draper. Went to Readdie's billet in the evening.

Tuesday 13th
Rain. Took LGs for short route march. Ordered frills. Johnny, Shiney and Blackett to dinner. Rehearsed in wooden hut (Recreation Room) at 8 p.m.

Wednesday 14th
Route march. Went up to Maroc Garden City to rehearse 'If you Were the Only Girl in the World' with Shiney (the lady). Johnny

Blackett   Gill   P.D.R.   Holmes   Johnstone
17th June 1916

Pierrot troup – 1916.

and Blackett to dinner. Rehearsed with the men in the hut at 8.30 p.m. Summer-time introduced in France 11 p.m.

Thursday 15th
Lecture by Col. Sharpe RA at 6 p.m. Rehearsed in 1st Bde Rec. Room 9 p.m. Got the pom-poms and frills. Took Sgt. Paget (Pioneer Sgt.) to the hut to arrange the stage.

Friday 16th
Spent nearly all day at the hut. Rehearsed our miniature regimental band (I played side drum) at 3 p.m. Concert at 8 p.m. Most successful. Bosch balloon was looking at us.

Saturday 17th
Readdie's landlord took photos of pierrot troupe 11.30 a.m. [which later appeared in the *Daily Mirror* – 'Dancing to the music of the guns']. Went to Maroc in the afternoon to Cameron HQ. Tea with their LGO. Also saw Black Watch LGO (Murray-Menzies).

Sunday 18th
Met 17th Welsh (Bantam Division)[37] at 11 a.m. Took over LGs in front line in Edgware Road in afternoon. Tea with Doc Ritchie at No. 1 FA in Garden City out of a china cup. Very good tea. Stayed with Motor MG officer and A Coy at the bottom of the Garden City. Currants and gooseberries in the garden.

Monday 19th
Brewster MMG relieved by Humphries MMG. Saw proof of photo. Official wind up about Bosch cutting wire. Arranged for 2 LGs in Reserve, afterwards cancelled. Dinkie arrived back.

Tuesday 20th
Took ranges with 'Barr and Stroud'. Inspected new 'Jarvis and Clark MG Stand'. 18th Welsh LGO came to see me.

Wednesday 21st
18th Welsh relieved 17th Welsh. This Bantam Div. was being filtered in amongst us. [They afterwards took over the sector. The men were so small that empty SAA boxes had to be used both on the fire step and as a step to the fire trench.]

Thursday 22nd
Inter-company relieved. C came to my house.

Friday 23rd
Humphries MMG left us. Terrific rain storm and some thunder. Our cellar flooded. Aubrey and I shared one of the few remaining dry mattresses.

Saturday 24th
Went up to a 60lb TMOP[38] to learn the art of observing and correcting fire. Had LGs firing on gaps in Bosch wire, that the TM had cut, all night. All coys went up to the front line so I was left to myself.

Sunday 25th
Battn relieved by Northants. Watched 18-pounders cutting wire. Went to N Maroc. Lived with A Coy. Watched a strafe up north after dinner from an upper window.

Monday 26th
Went to Les Brebis in the evening to arrange about ammunition etc. Saw the new LGs. Watched strafe again. Very vivid. Went to an infantry OP with Elsie.

Tuesday 27th
Rehearsed for the Triangle Show that had been brought on again in a modified manner. Rain. Blackett came back from leave. Lunched at Rob's.

Wednesday 28th
Rehearsed the Show before Maj.-Gen. Strickland Div. Commander.
Lunch in the open. Called on Readdie.

Thursday 29th[39]
Quiet day, preparing stores etc. [As all the LG sections were going
over with their respective companies, I, being young and innocent,
asked CO if I could go over somehow. He said I could go with
Billie Barber (2nd in Command) as orderly officer.] The Sussex
had 2 companies tackling the Double Crassier as we attacked the
triangle from two points, one each side of the apex. Both COs and
both Adjts. were to remain in advanced HQ in the deep dug-out in
Middle Alley (3 entrances). Spent a hilarious evening.

Friday 30th
Left Maroc 6 p.m. Assembled in assembly trenches 8.45 p.m. Bosch
strafed the assembled company hard from 9–9.10 p.m. when he
slackened off. Several casualties before zero which was 9.10 p.m.
We left sap G when we saw the right party was in. The left party
were round the bend out of sight. Mines didn't go up in the right
places and the wire wasn't cut properly. Both we and the Sussex
suffered heavy casualties and our two parties couldn't join. Tried
to bind up Shiney in the Bosch front line. Experienced a weird
feeling at seeing Bosch notice boards and stumbling over dead
and groaning Bosch for the first time. Billie Barber sent me back
at 10.45 p.m. to report that the line could not be held and could
not get in touch with the left. Found Middle Alley being strafed
much worse than the Bosch's own front line. Found Shiney on a
stretcher in the bottom of the trench with his SBs[40] wounded and
a few panic-stricken wounded practically stamping on him in their
hurry to get past. Arrived at Battn HQ not nearly as brave as when
I started. After much disputing over phone the Battn was called
back in the small hours.

July

Saturday 1st
Absolute calm, peaceful and bright morning dawned. Relieved
by 1st Royal North Lancs. (2nd Bde), and some Middlesex from
another division at 5 a.m. Returned to N Maroc. Greeted by my
servant beaming who said they'd all heard I'd been killed. Slept
till lunch. Relieved by 1st South Wales Borderers (3rd Bde) at
9 p.m. Went to Petit Sains. Egerton-Green and Freeman were
killed. Edwardes missing (afterwards reported killed). Holmes

died of wounds. Aubrey Dickenson, who was left out and only in charge of carrying party, died of wounds. The following officers were wounded: Dinkie, Wadner, Warner, Bennett and Waller OP, and Munroe temporally wounded.

5 out of 17 officers untouched, 10 out of 35 LGs untouched[41].

Sunday 2nd
Went to Holmes' funeral at Noeux in Brady's car. Heard that Aubrey had died at Béthune.

Monday 3rd
Sent in Indent for LG and spare parts lost. Moved at 6 p.m. for Haillicourt. Messed with A and D. Delightful summer evening with trees and untouched cottages.

Tuesday 4th
Looked over the Church. Called on B and C at the Vicarage. Left for Marles-les-mines at 5 p.m. in the rain. Charming old lady and 2 daughters (former like Mrs Fosbrook) who sang to Peter Davis and myself in our billet. They also broached a bottle of their best red wine. Messed with HQ, A and B.

Wednesday 5th
Made up LG section to 59. Started instruction. 8 guns to run now instead of 4. Cpl. Booker (Hong Kong Police) made my Sgt. Heard that instead of staying here to rest and train we were to do some more pushing, probably in the Somme. We were to move this evening, but postponed till next day. Had a long talk with Rob in his billet.

Thursday 6th
Left for Lillers at 6.30 p.m. Dinner at the Commerce. Stokes in good form. Train left at 10.45 p.m. One 2nd class compt. for A and B officers.

Friday 7th
Arrived Candas about 6 a.m. Detrained and marched to Flesselles. Breakfast by the roadside about 7 a.m. Rained hard when we got in about 10 a.m. Rotten billet. We saw the landlady shooing the fowls out of what was to be our mess. Not feeling at all happy.

Saturday 8th
Fine day. Left at 7.25 p.m. for Frechencourt. Held up for an hour and a quarter to let the 3rd Bde go by.

Sunday 9th
Breakfast at 12 noon in an orchard at the back of our billet which was an estaminet. We had all slept in the billiard room. 2 officers on the table. Beautiful day and very warm. Moved suddenly at 3.50 p.m. for Bresle. Dinner on the ground in another orchard. Slept in long gable tents. Various people chased by other people while going to bed. The former being in a state of nudity.

Monday 10th
Beautiful day. Left Bresle at 9.50 p.m. Marched through Albert and passed 6″ Naval guns making horrible noise.

Tuesday 11th
Arrived Becourt Wood just outside Albert about 1 a.m. Passed a batch of prisoners being marched along. Cheered up a little. Went over the battlefield of July 1st in the afternoon. Fairly quiet but our guns going all day and night. Bosch strafed the Wood a little at night. Lived at Battn HQ.

Wednesday 12th
During all this move I had been training the new L Gun sections. Rather a difficult job. Gave them firing in the afternoon, but Gen. Davis (1st or 3rd Bde) had some ricochets around about him as he was walking along and told me to stop. Sent 2 guns up to the Camerons who were in front of us.

Thursday 13th
Fired LGs. Bosch strafed us just as we left.

Friday 14th
Bosch sent over new gas shells. SBs walked round with a bottle of ammonia for anybody to sniff. Several casualties. Less noise during the day.

Saturday 15th
Many rumours as to our movements. Saw Blackett's brother. Heathcott (a Capt.) and 2 subalterns arrived.

Sunday 16th
Fired LG with Smoke Helmets on. Dinner with A Coy. 3 new subalterns arrived.

Monday 17th
Moved up to Scott's Redoubt (on high ground between Becourt and Contalmaison).

Tuesday 18th
Went round the line by Bazintin le Petit Wood in the morning. Heard suddenly that we were to move up there. Moved at 8.45 p.m.

Wednesday 19th
Lived with B Coy. Disgusting trenches. Found dead Bosch amongst the rubbish at the blown-in end of the dug-out. Northants did a Show on our left. Dewhurst wounded.

Thursday 20th
Battn to take a trench on the ridge. Cancelled. Relieved by Black Watch. Maxwell sniped and wounded. Returned to Scott's Redoubt. Battn HQ house was an old Bosch dressing station. [It contained 50 beds. Ceiling, walls and floor boarded and the 1st two whitewashed. 3 staircases and a slope for stretchers with a windlass at the top.]

Friday 21st
Glorious morning. Had a wash in the sun. Felt a new man. Ambler got a cushy wound.

Saturday 22nd
Went to look at the trenches we were to take that night. Got back to lunch 3 p.m. Moved up 8.30 p.m, zero 12.30 a.m. (Sunday). Anzacs were to go for Pozières[42] on our left and 1st Bde the Ridge on our right.

Sunday 23rd
Appalling time. Sat in a trench the whole night waiting for the next shell with the Reserve LGs. The trenches were blocked with other Regiments who had lost their way and wounded all the time the show was going on. I spent most of the time binding up people and giving them brandy. Very bad show indeed. Much too hurriedly prepared, or so it seemed to me. Having nothing to do, had plenty of time to think. Moore (Adjt.) left in command. Went back to Scott's Redoubt. Col. Bircham died of wounds, Webb, Sherlock, Waller F.P, Purdon and Hancock killed. Sladen and Heathcote wounded. Heavy losses amongst other ranks.

Monday 24th
Relieved by Munsters (3rd Bde). Went back to Albert. Heard that CO had died of wounds. Hazeltine (who was 2nd in command when

I joined in November 1915) came over from GHQ. Lived with A Coy. OP Waller came back.

Tuesday 25th
Had a really good bath. Wakeley came over from 16th Battn, where he was posted after being wounded with TMs in the Loos area. Peter Davis to dinner. Heard we were to go out for at least a fortnight.

Wednesday 26th
Left for Franvillers at 10.30 a.m. Trouble with LG handcarts. Tyres came off and handles broke. [These carts are now used by GPO telephones on smooth London streets. That is all they ought ever to have been used for.] Lunch on roadside near Bresle. Delightful billet and garden. Lived with A. Went round to Gibb, who had been orderly officer at Bde for some months, after dinner.

Thursday 27th
Lorries provided for us to go into Amiens. Thoroughly good day. Came back laden with parcels in an ambulance.

Friday 28th
Rode over to see Darrington and Poole at the 13th Battn at Bresle. Very hot day.

Saturday 29th
Started early morning parades. Very hot.

Sunday 30th
Bde Church Parade in open 10.30 a.m. Brig.-Gen. Hubback distributed ribbons afterwards. (Elsie got MC for Triangle). Moved at 5.45 p.m. to a camp at Henencourt Wood. (III Corps HQ at H Château.)

Monday 31st
Parade in morning. My best Lewis Gunner that morning shot a signaller through ankle while instructing LGs. Played cricket for A Coy v SBs in afternoon. Very hot. Battn had night ops. I didn't go.

August

Tuesday 1st
Inspection by Lt.-Gen. Poultney GOC III Corps.

Wednesday 2nd
Inspection by Brigadier in morning. Went to Amiens by bus with Blackett. Returned by 2 ASC cars early for night ops.

Thursday 3rd
Big scheme for Battns, for signalling to planes. Fired on range but had to stop owing to ricochets. Fired revolvers for Nos. 1 and 2 LGs.

Friday 4th
Rehearsal for night ops to be carried out next night. Much strafing amongst the higher authorities. Cricket. Lewis guns v TMB.

Saturday 5th
Daylight rehearsal for night ops 3.30 p.m.–9.15 p.m.

Sunday 6th
Night ops 1.30 a.m. Moore badly strafed by Maj.-Gen. Strickland over LGs. Didn't affect me. Went to bed 6 a.m. Cricket in afternoon. Officers v Sergeants. Atkinson, new CO arrived.

Monday 7th
Fired LGs on aeroplane range. Met RFC men.

Tuesday 8th
Nothing to report.

Wednesday 9th
Blackett and I performed at Sussex open-air concert in the Wood. Met their CO Willett afterwards.

Thursday 10th
Rain. Parades cancelled. Kit inspection. JS Wilson took over A Coy.

Friday 11th
Misty morning. Played badminton after tea.

Saturday 12th
Misty morning. Sussex sports in the afternoon. Brig. and Div. band there. Gibb to dinner. Heard that we were to move to Becourt and on the Mametz Wood tomorrow.

Sunday 13th
Badminton in afternoon. Moved to Becourt. Arrived at Maxe Redoubt just above, after wandering through the wood, very late. Bivouacked. Slept in open in valise. Rain. [The only time I ever slept in valise without a roof.]

Monday 14th
Rain. Went up to Mametz Wood to look round. Came back by road with Doc Ward. Battn moved up in the evening and relieved the 13th KRRC. HFE Smith (Effie) and Jack Wormald (as 2nd in command) arrived.

Tuesday 15th
Strafed. Went round trenches W of High Wood[43] with Peter Davis and Sgt. Booker. Rain and strafe in afternoon. Cockerel killed. 60 casualties in 2 days. Wormald went sick.

Wednesday 16th
Rain. Went round front line again with Peter. Strafed up there. Took digging party up at night to deepen Argyle Trench. Sniped and strafed. Lost 3 Sgts. of the party so came back. Cursed by CO for coming back. Northants and Sussex did a Show.

Thursday 17th
Our guns going at it the whole day. Bosch strafed also. Absolutely fed up. Received 4 letters and 3 PCs, cheered up a bit. Good night's rest on staircase of Bosch dug-out.

Friday 18th
Felt better. Visited Northants HQ and LGO. LNL[44] did a daylight show at 2.45 p.m. Moved up to relieve LNL in the evening. HQ remained in Mametz Wood.

Saturday 19th
Lived with D Coy in reserve. Heard that we were to be relieved in the evening. Cancelled, so HQ came up to relieve LNL HQ in Mill Street. Spent all night running up and down between HQ and the front line coys. Nobody knew what was happening or going to happen. A Coy did a sort of show in which Wilson and Elsie were hit. Didn't know where the Bosch were.

Sunday 20th
The worst day of my life. Perfect hell. Shelled all day with everything up to 11″. Sent up in afternoon to help A and C

Coys. Lost haversack and field glasses. Expected to be relieved at 2.30 p.m. and waited every minute from then till 8.45 p.m. before Gloucesters arrived. Every time the sentries saw a leaf of High Wood move they said the Bosch were massing. Came out at 8.45 and drank a tumbler of neat whisky at Gloucester HQ. No untoward effect. Orders were to return to Becourt Wood, but LGs had to go to Mametz Wood to collect spare ammunition and handcarts. While there, Bosch drenched the wood with gas. Couldn't recognise LGs in gas helmets and they couldn't recognise me. Collected a few and returned to Becourt wood. Remainder of LGs spent the night in Mametz and came on next day. Stokes refused to leave his post when relieved as no officer with relieving party. He was killed. Walley and Johnstone died of wounds. Atkinson (CO), Mitchell, Doc Ward and Hallett wounded.

Monday 21st
As all seemed quiet, went up to Mill Street to look for haversack etc. Not to be found. Wormald came back. Doc Collier arrived. Visit from Bulkely Hughes and Paul from 12th Battn.

Tuesday 22nd
Quiet day. Took HQ Coy to baths in Albert in the morning.

Wednesday 23rd
Started training new LGs. Lunch with D Coy. Dinner with C Coy. Gibb was there. Col. Abadie arrived.

Thursday 24th
Walked over to 9th KRRC transport lines through Becordel. Saw Howard Bury. Watched a strafe in the distance. Tea with C Coy. Hallett returned.

Friday 25th
Tea and listened to band at Bde GHQ at Maxe Redoubt. Hallett went back to hospital.

Saturday 26th
Went to 8th KRRC transport to look for Chug Chambers. He hadn't yet joined them. Saw the huge crater at La Boiselle.

Sunday 27th
Rain. Saw Chug after lunch. Moved to Mametz Wood 5 p.m.

Monday 28th
Went round the line with Blackett and Smith in afternoon. Just as we were finishing dinner in the open three shells arrived simultaneously and blew out the acetylene lamps. We all made a dash for the entrance to the dug-out but got on top of it instead of inside. A Coy had a lot of men buried by shells.

Tuesday 29th
Spent most of the day in dug-out. Thunderstorm in evening.

Wednesday 30th
Very wet and dull. Tea with A and C Coys. Heard about another show which had been put off.

Thursday 31st
Heard we were to take over High Wood and to the left of it. I went up early. Relief postponed owing to strafe. Lived in a little hole with steel rails overhead in a hollow near Mill Street with C Coy.

September

Friday 1st
Fairly quiet. We had a strafe at 6.30 p.m.

Saturday 2nd
Lot of strafing. Relieved by 1st Bde at about 6 p.m. Went to Blackwood between Albert and Becourt. Gott[45] and Bristowe arrived. Lived in tents.

Sunday 3rd
Big push taking place all round. Heard that we were to go back to the line once again and divisions would not be relieved till the 11th. Alarmed by shells falling across the road after dinner. Sounded nearer then they were.

Monday 4th
Heard we were to go back in support tomorrow. More shells in the same place. Went to Albert with Doc Collier to buy chocolate.

Tuesday 5th
Moved up to Mametz Wood. Awful mud. Tried to fix LD[46] horses and pack ponies to LG carts. All but 2 bolted and upset grooms and

carts. No damage, but decided on manpower. Heard that Johnny had died of wounds.

Wednesday 6th
Our guns at it all day. Very little Bosch retaliation. Tea with A Coy.

Thursday 7th
Beadell arrived in the morning. Looked for KOYLI Redoubt to see demonstration of rockets but couldn't find it. Moved to front line Wood Lane in evening on right of High Wood.

Friday 8th
Heard that if 3rd Bde succeeded in High Wood today we were to attack tomorrow. Lived with D Coy behind the Bank in large tree trunk shelter. 3rd Bde failed and Bosch used *flammenwerfer*. It looked as if High Wood was on fire. Gott left for 4th Army Infantry School, Flexicourt. Lucky man.

Saturday 9th
In spite of 3rd Bde failure, we attacked at 5.45 p.m. Blackett hit by premature Mills bomb 5 minutes before zero. Got him away in time. I went out to relieve Lee (C Coy) who was raving mad threatening everybody with revolver. Moore persuaded him to retire down the line. Dug hard all night. Never saw so many mangled Bosch lying about. They must have suffered very heavy losses. Hawke and Langton died of wounds. Holmes (attached MGC), Fison, Lee, Sneddon and Beadell wounded. Attack successful.

Sunday 10th
Jumbo Munroe wounded. Bristowe Smith and I left to run the whole front line. Lived on chocolate and brandy until Green (Smith's servant) brought a tongue and bottle of whisky. Relieved by 4th RB New Zealand who had wind up. Went back to transport field near Becourt Wood.

Monday 11th
Quiet day. Rested. Shells in distance only.

Tuesday 12th
Paraded in dark at 4.30 a.m. and marched to Baizieux. Tiny bedroom in the roof of a cottage. Hazeltine and CO 1st Battn lunched. Barrand arrived.

Wednesday 13th
Faman arrived. Wandered through charming glades and château garden. Delightfully peaceful.

Thursday 14th
Tea with Gibb at Bde. Went to a concert at Henencourt with Mason (Sussex, Bde Scout Officer) in Gilchrist's (Div. Sig. Off.) car. III Corps Padre mistook me for a Padre because at that time we wore the black Maltese Cross in our caps.

Friday 15th
3-weeks' training programme came out. Started training. Walked to Warloi in evening. Very peaceful and view reminded me of Blackgang, Isle of Wight. Saw prison's cage. Lee (another one) arrived. Heard good news about a new push[47].

Saturday 16th
Heard that our rest was to be cut off and that we should move next day. Later that we should *not* move. Listened to Div. Band playing at Bde after dinner. Brig.-Gen. thanked us for our Show at Wood Lane.

Sunday 17th
Church parade at Sussex camp with their drum and pipe band. Forrest and Bellance at lunch. Hazeltine and Jock Lloyd (APM) to lunch. Heard that we were to go up the line on Tuesday.

Monday 18th
Rain all day. All hoped order re move would be cancelled again. No luck. Dinner with Readdie.

Tuesday 19th
More rain. Left for Lozenge Wood near Fricourt at 1.15 p.m. Most uncomfortable. Slept under a draughty tarpaulin. Very cold and very noisy.

Wednesday 20th
Heard that we were to go back to Black Wood. Cheers! We should have tents and valises there. Moved in afternoon.

Thursday 21st
Smith came back. A few shells in the old place. Somewhat disturbed our night. A bomb store blew up.

Friday 22nd
Saw my first tank[48] on the Albert Road (a male). Walked round Albert and saw the Rly. Station. Col. Ward to dinner. Heard that Doc Ward and Johnny had got the MC.

Saturday 23rd
Went up to look round the line. [The whole time that we had been on the Somme we had always been fighting uphill and had never seen more than 200 yards of Bosch country in front of us. The big push of September 15th had gained the whole High Wood Ridge and we now saw a wonderful panorama of Bosch country with green trees and fields unbroken by shell holes.] Saw Flers and Martinpuich in the distance. Saw 5 more tanks. Anson arrived.

Sunday 24th
Heard that we were to go in front line again on Monday. Expected it would only be support or reserve. Some shells round about us during the day and night.

Monday 25th
Moved up to Flers Line at 3.15 p.m. A long dreary walk in mud past 'The Cough Drop'. Relieved Black Watch. Arrived about 10 p.m.

Tuesday 26th
3 a.m. bombed down the trench towards Eaucourt L'Abbaye for about 90 yards. Got 5 prisoners whom I searched at Battn HQ. Faman wounded. Went to help Ballance with B Coy. 2nd bombing show 11 a.m. 3rd and 4th at 6.30 p.m. and 11 p.m. Bristowe wounded in evening.

Wednesday 27th
Spent the night and morning with Forrest and Effie in the Cross Trench just captured. It led to the New Zealanders. Most curious situation. Some trenches led to the Bosch and others to our other divisions. Attacked the Bosch again at 2.15 p.m. Ballance killed and Anson wounded. Another attack with the Northants helping; partly over the top and partly along trench at 6.30 p.m. Really didn't know what I was doing by then. Neither of these two seemed successful.

Thursday 28th
Looked after the remains of B and C Coys and LGs. Thought Bosch meant to counter-attack on our left (Sussex and LNL) but

53

they didn't. Watched a Bosch directing 5.9" with red and green rockets. Red meant nearer me and green meant further away. A preponderance of red. Relieved by 19th London (47th Div.) at 11 p.m. Awful journey home through mud. The night was so dark that even lying on the ground nothing stood out against the sky. Not even the stumps of High Wood. Wandered about absolutely lost with a handful of men struggling along behind. Asked stray gunners in their gun pits where we were but they didn't know. Eventually recognised a dump of Bosch stick grenades and barbed wire coils by Worcester Trench and followed that to the Bank. Then on to Mill Street where a horse was waiting for me. When Effie arrived at the same spot he looked round and found *one* man following him.

Friday 29th
Got back to Black Wood about 6 a.m. Slept till noon. Marched at 2 p.m. back to Millencourt, a muddy village behind Albert but thought it was heaven. Became OC 2 Coys (B and C) (also 2nd in command and junior platoon commander). Col. Abadie went on leave at 9.30 p.m. Knew that at last the Division was really going to rest. Effie, Forrest and myself were the only officers left apart from HQ.

Saturday 30th
Faman returned. Called on Readdie after tea.

October

Sunday 1st
Church Parade with the Northants and their military band. (Not drum and pipe.) Clocks put back. Took the handcarts (empty) to Frenchencourt Rly Head. Managed to push the men onto lorries after giving them some tea at a canteen and rode back in the dark by myself musing and marvelling at my being over the ground instead of under.

Monday 2nd
Rain. Called on Readdie. Cold and very wet.

Tuesday 3rd
Rain. Paraded 5.45 a.m. and marched to main Albert–Amiens road to embus. The buses (French ones that I recognised off the Paris streets) eventually started at 11.15 a.m. Went through Amiens,

Flexicourt and Abbeville. Wonderful seeing shops and smartly dressed women again. Arrived Valines (between Abbeville and Le Tréport) at 9 p.m. Inhabitants awfully good to us. Delightful billet with 'Chambre de Toilette' attached. Good mess.

Wednesday 4th
Rain in morning. Discovered piano at an *auberge*. 1st four men went on leave. Lewis guns arrived (without their carts, thank the Lord) by lorry.

Thursday 5th
Went to Feuquières to get Battn money. Paid out. Told to send LGs to Gamarches (Rly Head) to fetch handcarts. Thought I'd got rid of them for good.

Friday 6th
6 new officers (non-riflemen) arrived (5 Northants and 1 5th Sussex) who received a very cold welcome from the Adjt. (Moore). Ommaney arrived. Gibb, who was now a Cameron Highlander, was lent to us and took over C Coy. I returned to my beloved LGs and started training again.

Saturday 7th
Went with Doc Collier to Abbeville by passenger train. Gott came back. Rob went on leave and I nominally took over his job. RQMS[49] Crabtree actually did the work. Waters arrived.

Sunday 8th
Drizzle. Church parade.

Monday 9th
Abadie came back. Forrest and Effie to dinner. Arranged a concert and went with Gibb and Doc to the *auberge* to rehearse. Buron (one of the non-riflemen) came to us as he stated that he could 'do George Robey'[50].

Tuesday 10th
Wormald and Moore went on leave. Took over the job of Adjt. Rehearsed at the inn. Decided to postpone concert till Monday.

Wednesday 11th
Went to Abbeville to buy lingerie etc. for concert (proposed being a girl). Rehearsed in evening.

Thursday 12th
Cherry arrived. Went to Chepy (next village) for lecture on 'Sanitation'. Rehearsed.

Friday 13th
Lecture by Campbell on PT at Chepy. Didn't go. Div. Band played on the village green. Asked the Div. Padre to lunch. Col. Bethel (Northants), Col. Willett (Sussex) and Isaacs (Bde Major) to dinner.

Saturday 14th
Rugger v LNL. Rehearsal in evening. Dobby (GSOI) came to lunch and lectured after in the village school.

Sunday 15th
8 GS wagons took party to Le Tréport for a 'bean feast'. Rehearsal.

Monday 16th
Concert in barn at 8.30 p.m. CO and Isaacs were there. Small house but appreciative.

Tuesday 17th
Route march to St Valery[51] a quaint village at the mouth of the Somme. Very enjoyable. Concert again in the evening but very few turned up and even all the performers didn't appear. Tired after the march was the excuse. Very wet night.

Wednesday 18th
RSM Saunders took Battn in Battn Drill. CO's conference re promotions. Night ops. CO's gramophone, a better one than ours, arrived. Ommaney left.

Thursday 19th
Bde Route march left with Gibb at 1 p.m. in ambulance for Chepy. Lorry at 3.30 p.m. from there to Gamarches. Train left there 5.30 p.m. Changed at Abencourt. Left there about 8.45 p.m. in 3rd class carriage with a drunken Poilu[52]. Amusing and not objectionable.

Friday 20th
Arrived Rouen 1 a.m. Slept together in the one remaining double bed at Hotel d'Angleterre. Left 9.45 a.m. in Paris–Havre express. Arrived Havre 11.30 a.m. Lunch at Hotel de Normandie, also dined there. Went to a cinema. Arrived at the Quay at 9.15 p.m. Got a cabin and went to sleep. Boat left 11.30 p.m.

Saturday 21st
Arrived Southampton on SS *St Petersburg* (GER). Train left 8.30
a.m. Arrived Waterloo 10.45 a.m.

Third Leave

Monday 30th
Left Waterloo 4.30 p.m. with Gibb. Arrived Southampton 6.50
p.m. No boats sailing so left Southampton West 8.30 p.m. Arrived
Waterloo 10.30 p.m.

Tuesday 31st
Arrived Waterloo 4 p.m. RTO sent us away.

November

Wednesday 1st
Went to Waterloo 4 p.m. Heard unofficially that no boats would be
likely to run so came away. Heard afterwards that a boat started
but was called back.

Thursday 2nd
Left Waterloo 4.30 p.m. Arrived Southampton 6.35 p.m. Left on
SS *Queen Alexandra* at 8.15 p.m. Very crowded. Slept in the
smoking room.

Friday 3rd
Arrived Havre in early morning. Told to stop on board and go on
to Rouen by boat. Breakfast 5 a.m. Went up the Seine and arrived
Rouen 5.30 p.m. Went to an English Revue at St Georges Hall.
Stayed at the Hotel d'Angleterre.

Saturday 4th
Went to the Cathedral and Church of St Joseph. Went to the Rive
Gauche Rly Station 1.15 p.m. Told to get food as the journey would
be long. Shunted onto siding at Romes Camp 10.30 p.m. Spent the
night in the train.

Sunday 5th
Left Romes Camp 10.30 a.m. via Amiens to Albert. Got out of train
just before Albert as there was a block and walked along line to the
station. Found the Battn at Albert where they had arrived from
Bresle that afternoon.

Monday 6th
Shared billet with Gibb. Shelled and bombed a little. Our guns quite as disturbing as the Bosch. HQ mess was the first I had ever had with a WC with water and in order.

Tuesday 7th
Rain. Lecture by Moore. McCabe and Dawson arrived.

Wednesday 8th
Div. Band in the cinema 5.30 p.m. Played the cornet in HQ mess but Bosch came along and stopped it with bombs.

Thursday 9th
Night ops. McCabe to hospital.

Friday 10th
Went round the line on left of Eaucourt L'Abbaye and saw Butte de Warlincourt. Bus to Fricourt. Came here via Contalmaison in an RFC tender towing a derelict plane. Saw Sussex about a piano. Bosch m. gunned the streets from planes.

Saturday 11th
Div. Band and cinema at 6 p.m. Merry dinner with B and C but went to sleep towards the end.

Sunday 12th
Took party to Church parade in cinema but it was full up so brought them back. Went to the evening service.

Monday 13th
Prepared for concert but found ASC in possession in cinema. Padre showed me an ASC workshop but was no good.

Tuesday 14th
Moore went as instructor to Div. School at Frechencourt. I took over Adjt.

Wednesday 15th
Col. Philipps (LNL) to dinner. Our little band played. Saw the RE 'Ideal Trenches' at Fricourt.

Thursday 16th
Concert in cinema 6 p.m. Full house. Bad programme. Revolver shooting in a cellar in afternoon.

Friday 17th
Bombs and shells in early morning closer than usual. Prepared to move to Bazintin tomorrow. Very cold.

Saturday 18th[53]
Move cancelled. Little snow. Much excitement over an alleged spy. Put him in the guard room. CO stayed in bed.

Sunday 19th
Moved to Bazintin 9.30 a.m. Arrived 12 noon. Slept in Nissen huts for first time. Quite comfortable. AA & QMG (Tulloch) came to see us.

Monday 20th
Picked up a bit of stained glass from the ruins of B. le Petit church. CO and OC Coys went round the line.

Tuesday 21st
Went to see Wallington (Staff Capt.). Saw our ration limbers held up in a traffic block so got a special permit from Traffic Officer to get them through. Effie left for 4th Army School, Flexicourt.

Wednesday 22nd
Wormald went to hospital again. Took over Flers Line near Eaucourt L'Abbaye from 10th Gloucesters. Lived in a 4.5" How. gun pit with live ammunition. Greeted on arrival by a salute of 5.9".

Thursday 23rd
Peaceful day. Brig.-Gen. and Bde Major came round at 5 p.m. Bde Pioneer Officer also came. Padre came up to see about burying all the bodies lying about.

Friday 24th
Little rain. 2nd Welsh officer came to look round. Langridge returned. Gerrard and Golding left.

Saturday 25th
Misty day so explored. Went down the vaults and tunnels of the Abbaye. Played a piano left there by the Bosch. Got inside derelict tanks.

Sunday 26th
More rain. Disgusting mud. Shelters fell in.

Monday 27th
Relieved by 2nd Welsh. Went back to tents at the side of Mametz Wood with CO. Lost our way. Ambler arrived back.

Tuesday 28th
Rested. Very cold.

Wednesday 29th
Very cold. Band played. Dawson went on leave.

Thursday 30th
Went to Albert. Visited a new canteen. Brig. came round. Very cold. Faman fetched tent floor boards from Contalmaison Circus. They were the wrong ones and eventually caused a complete stoppage of the war while GHQ wanted to put Brig., CO, Faman and me under arrest. Most entertaining.

December

Friday 1st
Major-Gen. came round. Coy commanders went to Factory Corner (near Flers) to see the line. Freezing, fog and wind.

Saturday 2nd
Prepared for move next day.

Sunday 3rd
Relieved SWB[54] at Factory Corner. Unpleasant walk along the valley beyond High Wood. Expected to be shelled but were not – a state of mind very often far worse than actual shelling. The valley was long and had a bad reputation.

Monday 4th
REs strengthened the cellar.

Tuesday 5th
Sgt. Green badly hit. (He had been Mess Sgt. at the Tile Works, Sheerness when I was there). Sent off pigeons. Calthorpe (Bde Major) came up to sleep. Northants officers came up to look round.

Wednesday 6th
REs in trying to open up a new room found a dead Bosch. Our ration truck on the High Wood light railway blown up. Most unfortunate.

Thursday 7th
Wormald went off in the morning to arrange billeting. Relieved by Northants at 6.30 p.m. Went to High Wood East Camp. Laurence arrived and took over B Coy. All three Bdes now held the Div. Sector. We were on the right. We therefore were never further out than Battn in Reserve to Bde.

Friday 8th
Wet but cleared up later.

Saturday 9th
Bubbly Jock came in to see Doc about a trip to the S of France. Bathed at Bazintin Baths. Shelled all round but not exactly on us. Band played.

Sunday 10th
Attended Holy Communion in HQ Mess Hut. Trench-boards arrived for the camp.

Monday 11th
Relieved Sussex in Support in the old Flers Line. Good deep dug-out in the dangerous valley. 3 entrances.

Tuesday 12th
Snow and slush. Trenches falling in.

Wednesday 13th
Went round the companies. Readdie came in. Downes (OC Lowland Coy RE) came in.

Thursday 14th
No rain.

Friday 15th
Northants sent up advance party in broad daylight. Bosch strafed and killed Read my servant just as he was leaving the dug-out with my kit. He had been a most excellent servant for over a year. L/C Collet (Police Corp.) also killed and Langridge hit by the same shell (a 77mm). Relieved by Northants and went back to No. 2 Camp Bazintin le Petit. Dawson returned.

Saturday 16th
Shelled at night. One shell went through a man's trousers and blankets when he was asleep and had a bad burst under the floor.

Manwin injured. These were horrible Naval guns and very fast. No time to duck. (The man was not wearing his trousers).

Sunday 17th
Quiet and misty day. Col. Fortune (Black Watch) to dinner.

Monday 18th
McCabe returned.

Tuesday 19th
Frost. Very cold. Relieved Sussex at Factory Corner.

Wednesday 20th
Quiet day. Cherry rejoined.

Thursday 21st
Ordinary heavy rain. Inter-company relief.

Friday 22nd
Gale and rain.

Saturday 23rd
Cleared front posts for an artillery strafe. Relieved by Northants and went back to No.2 Camp.

Sunday 24th
Garrard and Golding returned.

Monday 25th
Open-air Christmas Service in morning. Col. Willett (Sussex) and Woodroffe (2nd in Command Sussex) to lunch. They and CO went on leave. Effie came back. Wormald left in command.

Tuesday 26th
CSM Chevis got his commission.

Wednesday 27th
Relieved Sussex in support area (the old Flers Line). Isaac (Bde Major) came back.

Thursday 28th
Quiet day. Much rain at night.

Friday 29th
5th Border Regt CO and Coy commanders came up to look round.

Saturday 30th
Strafed by 5.9″ but personally felt safe in dug-out. GOC 1st Bde came in.

Sunday 31st
Relieved by 5th Border Regt 157th Bde (Divisional relief). Went to No. 2 Camp again.

References

[1] Assistant Military Landing Officer.
[2] Lt. Robinson ('Rob') had the distinction of being the only officer who served continuously with the Battn from the outbreak of war until the Armistice. He became Capt. MC. *See* 11th November 1918.
[3] General Service.
[4] Quarter-Master's.
[5] Killed in April 1916, Loos.
[6] Killed in July 1916, Pozières.
[7] Killed in July, 1916, Loos.
[8] Small Arms Ammunition.
[9] i.e. Ravenscroft's old school.
[10] Killed High Wood, August, 1916.
[11] i.e. build up the top of the trench facing the enemy, usually with sandbags.
[12] There was no repetition of the informal Christmas Truce of 1914.
[13] Lewis Gun Officer.
[14] Presumably double-decked civilian buses taken over by the War Office.
[15] Royal Engineers.
[16] Rifleman's term for bayonet.
[17] Communication Trench.
[18] Army Service Corps.
[19] Royal Army Medical Corps.
[20] Joffre had since 2nd December 1915 been Commander-in-Chief of all the French forces and effectively responsible for the conduct of the war.
[21] Casualty Clearing Station.
[22] Ravenscroft is not strictly accurate. The Siege of Verdun, probably the bloodiest single military operation of the war, officially started on 21st February and lasted until July of the same year.
[23] Ravenscroft's middle name being Donovan, he was known as Don.
[24] Assistant Adjutant & Quarter-Master General, i.e. a Lt. Col. on the Divisional Staff, the Chief Administrative Officer.
[25] A natural embankment running into the German lines.
[26] The Germans had first used gas at the 2nd Battle of Ypres in April 1915.
[27] General Staff Officer with the rank of Colonel.
[28] Killed July 1916.
[29] Used for spraying areas affected by low-flying gas.
[30] Killed August 20th 1916 at High Wood.

[31] Field General Court Martial.

[32] A mine blown with the intention of destroying the enemy's underground galleries.

[33] Shell of a German 77mm gun, a very quick-firing weapon.

[34] Only recently introduced.

[35] A gas helmet made of cloth with glass eye-pieces and a tube valve. It went right over the head and the cloth was soaked in chemicals. Replaced by the box respirator at the end of 1916.

[36] Actually carried out on 30th June (*see* below)

[37] A Bantam Division consisted of men of short stature.

[38] Trench Mortar Observation Post.

[39] Ravenscrost's Battalion was not strictly speaking part of those forming the main British attack on the Somme further south and consequently the action has not been extensively treated in the literature.

[40] Stretcher Bearers.

[41] The British Army suffered 57,400 casualties on this day.

[42] The First Australian Division's attack on the village of Pozières was one of the few successful attacks during the Somme offensive (*Somme*, Lyn Macdonald, 1983).

[43] High Wood was the scene of some of the bloodiest fighting on the Somme, and the whole Western Front. It finally fell to the British on 15th September. (*Somme*, Lyn Macdonald, 1983).

[44] Loyal North Lancashire Regt.

[45] Known as 'Strafer' Gott, he became Lt. General in the 2nd World War and was shot down and killed in the Western Desert in August 1942.

[46] Light Draught.

[47] This was the day great gains were made with the aid of the tanks.

[48] Tanks were first used by the British with initial success on 15th September but half of the 36 tanks which went into action broke down. The 'male' tank carried two six-pounder cannons, the 'female' tank had four machine guns.

[49] Regimental Quarter-Master Sergeant.

[50] The famous music hall comedian.

[51] The 51st Highland Division surrendered here in 1940.

[52] French Private.

[53] The Battle of the Somme officially ended this day. Ten of Ravenscroft's sister Rifle Battalions had been engaged.

[54] South Wales Borderers

II

January 1st 1917 to December 31st 1917

1917

January

Monday 1st
Marched to Albert at 1.15 p.m. Oppy rejoined as 2nd in command.

Tuesday 2nd
Busy day in the Orderly Room.

Wednesday 3rd
Busy day. Dined with B and C Coys. Doc Collier went on leave.

Thursday 4th
WC Smith arrived. Started LG instruction.

Friday 5th
Mills bomb exploded while party were taking out fuses. 5 wounded. Sgt. Kelly died the following day. Went to a lecture by Corps. Court Martial officer.

Saturday 6th
Effie, Gibb and Chevis went on leave. Dined with A and D.

Sunday 7th
Church parade in cinema at 10 a.m. Our little band played us to church and played the service.

Monday 8th
Inspected Transport lines behind Albert in the afternoon with Oppy.

*A watercolour painted by D Neave (1st Division
RE) of High Wood as it appeared in the winter of
1916–17. The cross commemorates those of the 1st
Division who fell during the Battle of the Somme,
July – October 1916.*

Tuesday 9th
Went up to see Gloucester at Fricourt Farm. McDowell (Rhodesian)
arrived. Wormald left for England.

Wednesday 10th
Relieved 10th Gloucesters in Fricourt Farm. Camp moved at
12.30 p.m, arrived 2 p.m. McCabe and large party left for a
Musketry Course.

Thursday 11th
Lionel St Aubyn arrived as Transport Officer. Wasur rejoined.
Looked round C Camp on the other side of the road.

Friday 12th
Took over C camp from Indian Cavalry. Spotlessly clean. Worked
on drains and mud. Rain.

Saturday 13th
Prosecuted at FGCM at the School in Albert. Lunched at the Café.
A little show. CO and Rob (QM) returned from leave.

Sunday 14th
Gill and Williams went on leave. A few shells (HV) but not very close. Raided with RSM the gamblers' den.

Monday 15th
Gott returned from leave. One latrine blown up by HV shell at night. Too close to be amusing.

Tuesday 16th
Walked to Pozières with the CO to find our 1st Battn. They had left the day before. Pozières was absolutely flat, just the open road with a wooden hut or two. The notice board stating that it was Pozières was the only means of knowing when we got there. Heavy fall of snow. More shelling at night. Large hole (8-inch probably) 7 yards from Sgts.' Mess. No casualties.

Wednesday 17th
Doc Collier returned from leave. Muscat (late of Melton Militia) arrived. More snow and shelling at night.

Thursday 18th
Another musketry party, 200 strong, left at 8.45 a.m.

Friday 19th
A quiet day.

Saturday 20th
Fired LGs with B Coy.

Sunday 21st
Doc Ward rejoined. Gracie arrived. Doc Collier transferred to 1st Gloucesters (3rd Bde). Very cold.

Monday 22nd
Very cold. Went to Gas lecture in cinema at Albert with Gibb and Gott. Had tea with Airth (TMB) and went to cinema at 5 p.m.

[It was so cold during these days that we dressed when going to bed and undressed slightly when we got up. Breath froze on 'flea bag' and looking-glass when shaving. Laurence and Gott made most excellent rum punch in the evenings.]

Tuesday 23rd
Balloon broke loose and was tossed about for over an hour before it drifted northwards out of sight. Sometimes the basket was flung

right on top of the envelope. One man descended in a parachute, but it seemed as if another stayed in the basket[1]. Bosch planes flew over us. Australian billeting party arrived. Intensely cold.

Wednesday 24th
Just as cold. Moved to Bresle at 10 a.m. Bomb dropped just between A and D Coys in the road while marching through Albert. No damage. Arrived Bresle about 1.45 p.m. Vicars joined. Coy officers in draughty wood and canvas huts. I luckily had a tiny room in the mayor's house. CO had kitchen underneath so was warm.

Thursday 25th
Orderly room in a corner of the village school room. Most difficult to wash while Mlle was teaching small children geography and the iniquity of the Germany People. The school room was the only warm place in the village. Vicars went on leave.

Friday 26th
Prosecuted at FGCM in a case of Desertion. Inspector of Schools arrived and nearly sacked the school mistress for allowing us in the school room. Kelly arrived. Managed to persuade Mlle to allow us to remain until we could find another. The village was packed with troops and there was not a single room to move to.

Saturday 27th
Route march through Franvillers, Baizieux, Warloy, Henencourt. Very pleasant. Saw Danny Maher as Bde Major of another Bde. He was our Transport Officer when I first joined. Lecture by Brig.- Gen. Hubbard in the Church.

Sunday 28th
After searching the whole village with the Interpreter, managed to get YMCA superintendant's sitting room for Orderly Room. Dined at Bde HQ, asked if I should like to be attached to Bde as a 'Learner'. All sorts of visitors to lunch. Charles Ambler and Lindsay returned.

Monday 29th
Did a scheme with LNL. Boxing competition at 5 p.m. Moved into a new Orderly Room.

Tuesday 30th
Div. Band played in the Square in the afternoon. Our band augmented by piccolo, oboe and extra bassoon, played at mess.

Wednesday 31st
Bde Route March Henencourt, Warloy, Vardencourt, Contay, Franvillers. Gibb took me to Amiens in an ambulance, Laurence, Fewtrell, Effie and Kafir Smith came too.

February

Thursday 1st
Went to live at 2nd Bde. Laurence had gone there a day or two before. Doc Ward and 3 colonels to dinner. Visited 141 FA about powder for Trench Feet at Lavieville. Tea with MG Coy.

Friday 2nd
Tea with CO in his bedroom.

Saturday 3rd
Bde moved to Mericourt-s-Somme. I settled claims in Bresle Village with Interpreter. Rode by myself on a push bike through Ribemont, Mericourt L'Abbé, Sailly Laurette, Cerisy, Morcourt, Mericourt-s-Somme. Met PL Forward (Harrow) on the way.

Sunday 4th
General in bed. Arranged massed bands with Tulloch (AA & QMG).

Monday 5th
Bde moved to Chuignes. Rode Kitty and went on ahead to catch up Laurence who was doing the billeting at Chuignolles as well. Slept in the school with Bde Scout Officer Allan (LNL) who smoked cigars in bed before breakfast. Messed in a farmhouse.

Tuesday 6th
Cleared up the surroundings after the French had gone. DADOS[2] came in with calico to be made into night shirts for patrolling in the snow.

Wednesday 7th
Took samples of snow sheets to Sussex and Northants at Chuignolles. Felt like a Commercial Traveller. Relieved 108th French Regiment. Excellent dinner with champagne in a dug-out in the Quarry in the Bois de Boulogne near Belloy. Brought up the Bde Transport through Dompière and Assevillers (Right sector). The front line ran roughly from Villers-Carbonnel to E of Flaucourt.

Thursday 8th
Very comfortable and *warm*. Quiet and sunny. The Division had given strict orders that no movement was to be made above ground in daylight, as in the past when we relieved the French in a quiet sector we had always advertised the fact to the Bosch and before a week was out the sector lost its tranquillity.

Friday 9th
Gotir, a Frenchman who had been left behind till we were settled, left. Tea with 23rd and 26th. Field Coy RE on the opposite side of the Quarry.

Saturday 10th
Corps and Army to lunch. Tea with Battn HQ in the line, met VB Hill whom I had met at Sheerness.

Sunday 11th
1st Bde to lunch. In spite of above Div. orders, the 6th Welsh (Div. Pioneers) dug trenches (acting under Div. orders, of course) in broad daylight. This led to the Bosch strafing on Tuesday.

Monday 12th
Calthorpe (RE) arrived to take over Bde Major.

Tuesday 13th
Isaac (Bde Major) left for GSO II 50th Div. Much strafing of the quarry in the morning. My bucket buried.

Wednesday 14th
Relieved by 1st Bde. Back to Chuignes. Overtook RSM Saunders on a horse suffering from malaria (the RSM, not the horse).

Thursday 15th
Listened to RE peacetime band at Chuignolles. Thaw began.

Friday 16th
Thaw continued and mud started. Went round the transport lines with Wallington. Went over to Chuignolles to the Battn on business and stayed to tea.

Saturday 17th
Warm, damp and misty.

Sunday 18th
Nothing to report.

Monday 19th
Nothing to report.

Tuesday 20th
Rain all day. Dinner with 2nd TMB. Laurence went to III Corps HQ as Learner.

Wednesday 21st
Went round the 4 Battns in an ambulance doling out foot powder.

Thursday 22nd
Rode up with Wright and a Sussex officer to look for cellars and dug-outs in Dompière and Becquincourt in the morning.

Friday 23rd
Relieved 3rd Bde. Walked up with Wallington to well-arranged dug-outs on the Becquincourt–Herbecourt road (left sector).

Saturday 24th
Looked for suitable spot for SAA store. Sought assistance from Rly Construction Officer who lived in the area. Tea with Sussex HQ and saw an interesting old OP[3].

Sunday 25th
Sent James (my servant) to see Sussex MO.

Monday 26th
Went with Wallington to see new Bomb Store near Flaucourt. Walked through Herbecourt and called at Battn HQ. Major of 146th Bde arrived for attachment.

Tuesday 27th
Looked for accommodation for Northants and LNL. Major-Gen. Strickland to lunch.

Wednesday 28th
Walked over to LNL HQ in the morning.

March

Thursday 1st
Showed Pierson (Northants) where his billets were. He and his company were preparing to do a raid. Sunny day and much shelling all round, but not very close.

Friday 2nd
Nothing to report.

Saturday 3rd
Tea and dinner with Battn. Met Heberden who had just come out.
He was at Fort Dorland, Chatham and Sheerness with me.

Sunday 4th
Quiet day. A 'chinese' (i.e. feint) attack to annoy the Bosch. Very
little retaliation. Snow fell during the night.

Monday 5th
Went round 3 Battns with Calthorpe. Northants did their raid at
night. No prisoners.

Tuesday 6th
Went to Flaucourt Bomb Store with Wallington. A dear old man
(Sussex) was in charge. He always referred to me as 'the Lieuten-
ant'. Heard that I was to be attached to the 25th Bde RFA.

Wednesday 7th
Walked with the new Bde Padre to Chuignes to report to the
Gunners. Only their wagon lines there. Advised by them to
report to their CO in the morning. Went on to a house where
Cherry, Golding and Dawson, who had been left out of the line,
lived. Had a bath at the new baths built by Ford, an American
and an MO of one of the Div. Medical Staff. He became famous
in the Div. on account of his baths. Fed and slept with the 3
above-mentioned officers.

Thursday 8th
CO and Blacknett arrived. Went up to Dompière in CO's car and
reported to Lt.-Col. Lewin commanding 25th Bde RFA at the Mill.
Good deep dug-outs. Oppy and Charles Ambler wounded in the
Battn – Ambler v. badly.

Friday 9th
Went round OPs with Lewin. Saw the camouflaged tree, a steel
ladder encased in painted canvas. It was made by the French
and it was an exact copy of a dead tree stump. The tree was
removed and the imitation put in its place in one night. Snow
fell so we didn't go up it. Tea with Shanks (commanding 26th
Coy RE). Played on their piano which was the piano left by the

Bosch in Eaucourt L'Abbaye. The sappers had got it out of the vaults, carried it 300 yards through mud to the light railway and had carried it about ever since. The dug-out looked exactly like a woman's boudoir.

Saturday 10th
Read the 'Retreat from Mons' and didn't go out. My kit arrived after wandering round.

Sunday 11th
Toured with Kew (the Adjt. of 25th Bde). Visited 114 Battery, Central Exchange, and lunched with 113 Battery. Very clear day. Met Faman in Martinique Avenue.

Monday 12th
Left Bde and went to 114 Battery RFA (18 pounders) at Assevillers in the afternoon.

Tuesday 13th
Went up the camouflage tree.

Wednesday 14th
Went to various OPs with Major MacClaverty (OC).

Thursday 15th
Bright day. Watched gun laying and firing.

Friday 16th
Misty morning. Went to Tree OP with Rallin in the afternoon and fired the guns from there by telephone.

Saturday 17th
Bosch cleared out of their lines.[4] Infantry followed up the banks of the Somme. We moved up the guns at night to the left of Belloy. Wonderfully quiet. Many fires burning behind the Bosch lines. Much difficulty with the guns in the mud.

Sunday 18th
Walked through Villers-Carbonnel and along old Bosch line looking at our line from their point of view. The tree OP was perfect. Saw a tank trap on the main road. This was merely a huge pit dug in the road with felled trees hiding it from view. It was a beautiful day and one could see the woods in the far distance on the other side of the river. A wonderful feeling of elation and freedom. Not

a shot was fired. Met Doc Collier. Walked around the Boulogne Quarry with Kitty [i.e. Lt. Kitwood] in the afternoon. Warned about booby traps.

Monday 19th
Moved to the Priory which the Bosch had tried to destroy. This was a fine old building on the banks of canal which ran on the west side of the river. The Bosch had cut the banks, so the Priory was an island and the Rly Station beside it was under water. No room had more than 3 walls and therefore very draughty. Officers of all four battns lived with us and everyone very excited. Afterwards heard that the proper name for the 'Priory' was Happlincourt Château at Pont les Brie.

Tuesday 20th
Thought it time to find out what I should do as I felt in the way with the Gunners in their crowded position and all their guns were out of range, so went to lunch with Battn in the old front line dug-out. Met Humphrey Butter who had come as proper Adjt. Learnt nothing definite and heard that Bosch might not hold the Hindenburg Line.

Wednesday 21st
Explored old Bosch gun pits and found them smashed to bits by our shells. Found a Bosch automatic pistol and comic paper with low remarks and pictures about England. Walked most of the way to Chuignes via Villers-Carbonnel, Belloy, Assevillers and Dompière to the little 60th House. Found MacDowell, McCabe and Muscat there this time. The gunners all went back to their wagon lines at Chuignes. They were pretty crowded there too.

Thursday 22nd
Called on 114 Battery. No orders for me. Went for a stroll with Kitty. 2 short snowstorms.

Friday 23rd
Walked with St Aubyn to Cappy, Bray and Froissy. Shopped at Canteen at Bray. Cappy looked charming by the river. Discussed peace and how long it would take to get everything out of France. Astounded to hear that 2 years had been suggested.

Saturday 24th
Kitty came in and told me orders had come in that I should report to 26th Field Coy RE at Brie. Did so and passed Battn making

the main road on the way up. Went through Fay, Estrées, Villers-Carbonnel. Found Shanks still OC.

Sunday 25th
The main Amiens–Vermand road crossed the Somme on 5 bridges. The Bosch had blown up all 5, and in addition had diverted the stream by cutting through the road embankment. This meant 6 gaps which had to be repaired. All three Div. Field Coys were on this and the 26th had the gap included. The battns of the Div. were repairing the roads on each side of the river. The RE work was running in 3 shifts of 8 hours. Huge flares were used at night but not once did a Bosch plane come anywhere near.

I superintended working parties filling the gap with the bricks from the mass of ruins of the village of Brie. It would have probably caused us much more delay if the Bosch had left the houses standing and merely blown up the roads because we should have had no material for filling up in that case.

Monday 26th
Watched the progress of the bridges. No. 2 finished and the gap practically filled in. A dam of piles and concrete had to be made first to stop the stream rushing through. All the bridges when complete took the heaviest tanks. Wooden ones to take field guns and infantry in fours had been run up before I got there so that traffic could reach the other side. Snow and sleet.

Tuesday 27th
No. 1 finished. Girders of Nos. 3 and 6 put in position. Walked to top of hill across the river and looked at several lines with thick belts of barbed wire. These lines had a wonderful command of the crossings and the opposite slope and I felt very thankful that we hadn't been told to cross before the Bosch departed. Saw a damaged aeroplane. Caught in a snowstorm. No. 4 started at night.

Wednesday 28th
All bridges finished. Walked through Eterpigny to Péronne by road. Péronne was an amazing sight. The front of every house lay in a huddled mass in the road, thus ruining the houses and blocking the roads in one action. It reminded me of a series of dolls' houses with their fronts open. Listened to a band playing 'The Girl in the Taxi' in the Market Place. Walked home along the railway and saw numerous wagons burnt and others with the axle boxes removed – the body resting direct on the axles. At every join of the metals a small charge had been exploded, thus leaving

each rail with a jagged end and a gap of about eight inches from its neighbour.

Thursday 29th
Wet day. Lambert (Mess Pres.) went to Amiens. The Interpreter came back (from leave?).

Friday 30th
Ordinary day.

Saturday 31st
Rly construction people cut the bank dividing the river and canal and also the bank dividing the canal from the railway in such a way that the water gradually left the railway and returned to the canal now at a lower level. Watched 23rd F Coy RE driving piles for No. 6 medium bridge. Each heavy bridge had a medium one built afterwards by its side to provide an up and down track.

April

Sunday 1st
Field Coys inspected by CE III Corps in morning and congratulated on their achievement. Went for a walk along the railway towards Chauves and watched the jagged edges of the rails being cut off. They were filed half through and then put in a rail bender and bent till they snapped along the filing. Walked to St Christ and saw the bridges there. Came home along the canal bank and saw the barges that had contained forage burnt out. Moved into Nissen hut for messing. Padre came to dinner.

Monday 2nd
Medium Bridge No. 4 started.

Tuesday 3rd
Left to be attached to Div. HQ Q branch.[5] Lift in CE's (III Corps) car to Foucaucourt. Walked to Proyart, had tea in tea rooms there, and then on to Chuignolles. Slept in half a Nissen hut. Messed in A Mess (with Maj.-Gen.) in the Mayor's house. Lt.-Col. Holbrook was AA & GMG, Capt. Johnson was DAA & QMG and Major Clowes was DAQMG.

Wednesday 4th
Heavy snow. Went in open car with Clowes to Assevillers to see OC Dumps.

Thursday 5th
Spring day with showers. Stayed in the office looking at papers and digesting them. Lt.-Col. Pagan to dinner.

Friday 6th
Snow and sun alternately. Jock Lloyd APM[6] (from B Mess) to dinner. Maj.-Gen out.

Saturday 7th
Called on 114 Battery and found them all suffering from innoculation. Called on the Battn at Chuignes.

Sunday 8th
Went to see Town Major and 6th Welsh about accommodation.

Monday 9th
Dined with 114 Battery. Battle of Arras [7] began but didn't affect us.

Tuesday 9th
Went over to see Battn who had just come back to Chuignes having finished the road. Met Laffer, an LG who had been wounded last summer. Extraordinary weather. Fierce hail storms.

Wednesday 10th
Dined with 2nd Bde HQ. Played bridge.

Thursday 11th
Ordinary day.

Friday 12th
Went in car with Johnson to Morcourt and Mericourt-s-Somme to see about billeting. Col. Abadie and Col.Coghill to dinner. Beautiful day. Holbrook came back from instructing another Div.

Saturday 13th
Soccer and rugger mixed match. 1st Div. officers v 2nd Bde Officers (changed rules at half-time). Very amusing. Result – lost soccer 0–3, won rugger 12–8. Chichester Constable arrived. Dinner with Battn HQ.

Sunday 14th
Went to church in evening.

Monday 15th
Moved to Mericourt Château. Garden running down to the Somme.
Went in car with Clowes to Brie, Mons (close by), Athies, saw huge
craters at the crossroads, Doingt, Péronne, tea with 3rd Bde and
then home.

Tuesday 16th
Autumn weather. Tea with 26th Field Coy in Mericourt. Played
the same old piano from Eaucourt L'Abbaye.

Wednesday 18th
Russel Brown CRE and Gilchrist (Div. Signal Officer) to dinner
from B Mess. Band played. The mess at the Château was a
fine big room but rather bare. The officers' and junior officers'
bedrooms were huts built by the French in the grounds. Played
rope quoits after tea.

Thursday 19th
Went to see Transport of 2nd Bde units at Morcourt. GOC went
on leave. Tea with 2nd TMB. Dinner with Blackett (C Coy). Our
band played.

Friday 20th
Spring morning. Walked to Etinghem along the river. Delightful.

Saturday 21st
Stayed in most of the day. My chief duty now was answering the
telephone as the Div. was doing nothing. Went to Chuignolles in
closed car with Holbrook in evening. Met the nephew of Douglas of
Motorbike fame. He had been at Ferfay on the Lewis Gun Course
with me. He is now in RFC.

Sunday 22nd
Played rugger for officers of the Battn against officers of Sussex.
Met RSM Blenkin who was at Scoules (Sheppey) with me. He had
just come out. We won 18–8. Tea with Sussex HQ.

Monday 23rd
Walked along bank of Somme canal to Chipilly and Cerisy in
the afternoon. Saw the IWT[s] travelling at leisure on their
barges. Quite hot.

Tuesday 24th
Walked to Proyart in the afternoon. Ran across the 2nd Bde
perspiring over a field day with Gunners and aeroplane. Cloudless

day. Bought some picture postcards by Leo Foutan. Had tea at Officers' tearoom.

Wednesday 25th
Asked Holbrook if I could go over to the Battn for a concert. 'You are always wanting to go to your Battn. Have you nothing to learn here?' was his reply. This angered me at first as all Staff Officers took the afternoon off every day as there was nothing to do. Anger turned to amusement later. However, went over to the Battn. Pulled in Tug of War, Barnes (Rhodesian) arrived. Dobby (GSOI) told me that I'd better rejoin the Battn as there was nothing to do at Div. HQ and I might return to the G office when they went into the line. 1st Div. and Guards Div. now formed XIV Corps as GHQ reserve.

Thursday 26th
Walked to Proyart in afternoon and then on to Morcourt to rejoin the Battn.

Friday 27th
Went out with Battn through Chipilly training in the morning. Dinner with Blackett.

Saturday 28th
Butter sick (measles). Did Adjt.'s work as well as LG. Bde sports in the afternoon. LNL 1st, KRRC 2nd.

Sunday 29th
Most perfect day. CO and Effie went to Paris. Heard we were to move to Péronne tomorrow. 5 soccer matches with Black Watch. Butter to CCS. Forrest in command. Received various 'warning orders' and countermanded orders to move tomorrow.

Monday 30th
Received final definite orders from Bde at 1 a.m. when I was in bed, that we were to move at 8.30 a.m. Wrote out orders for OC coys, QM etc. while half asleep in bed. Marched at 8.30 a.m. to Bray. Entrained about 2.30 p.m. having arrived about noon and went via Merignolles (which we had passed en route for Bray in the morning), Chaunes, Pont les Brie, Péronne to Roisel. Arrived about 10.30 p.m. Forrest had to run after the train at Péronne where we stopped for half an hour or so. Much trouble detraining the horses at Roisel as there was no ramp. Very obliging RTO there. Slept on good grass in tents. Heard 2 shells.

May

Tuesday 1st
Fine day. Horses all enjoyed green grass in contrast to brown mud. Coalbox (a shetland pony; probably a pit pony and rescued by the Battn at Zillebache in 1914 or early 1915) thoroughly happy rolling in the grass. The Battn was to do the unskilled labour required to help the Canadian Rly Engineers in their relaying the Rly beyond Roisel. Started in the afternoon. Laurence came in to see us. He was Bde Major to a Bde in the neighbourhood.

Wednesday 2nd
Holbrook came up to see us. Laurence and his Bde staff came in in the evening.

Thursday 3rd
Ordinary day. Carried on LG classes.

Friday 4th
CO and Effie came back from Paris. Forrest went to Div. School. Went to the ADMS office of the 42nd Div. nearby to worry on the phone our Bde and Div. who were still miles away where we had left them, about leave to Paris for Blackett and myself.

Saturday 5th
Brig.-Gen., Wallington and Calthorpe came to tea. CO missed them. Heard that leave had been granted to us about 10 p.m. Made frantic efforts to get some sort of conveyance to Amiens (about 36 miles away) in time to catch the 12.30 p.m. express to Paris next day, as if we missed that we should miss the opera and there would not be another performance during our 3 days sojourn. Can. Rly RE's said they might have a Ford going to Péronne at 8 a.m. next morning. No trains available.

Sunday 6th
Fine bright morning. Left in the Ford at 8.30 a.m. with Sheep-shanks who was going on English leave and arrived at Péronne about 20 minutes later. Called on everybody likely to have a car there but failed. Started walking to Villers-Carbonnel. Blackett went into a station just outside Péronne (La Chapellette) to ask about trains while I stayed on the road to stop any car. The RTO[9] with a somewhat original sense of humour told him 'Oh yes, he could get to Amiens by 12.30 – tomorrow, ha, ha, ha'. Didn't appreciate the joke. Hailed a closed Daimler who stopped. A Brig.-

Gen. RA inside alone. Very decent and gave us a lift to Villers-Carbonnel. Started walking along the main road that our Battn had re-made a fortnight before. Very hot and getting on for 11 a.m. Hailed an RFC tender. Only the driver and some old tyres inside. Asked him if he could get to Amiens by 12.15 p.m. Said he'd do his best. Went all out over bumps at the fastest RFC speed. Puncture within sight of Amiens Cathedral. Arrived at the Station at 12.05 p.m. Met Merriot (who was in the same lodging house as I at Cardiff) and arrived Paris 4.15 p.m. Stayed at the Continental. Dinner at Café de Paris. Went to *Samson & Delilah*.

Monday 7th
Lunch at Armonsville in the Bois. Car to Versailles and St Germain. Dinner at Café de la Rue. Olympia.

Tuesday 8th
Lunch Ambassadeurs, Champs Elysées. Notre Dame, Invalides, Montmartre, dinner at Café de Paris and met Isaac there. Théâtre Mayoc.

Wednesday 9th
Lunch Café de Paris. Left Gare du Nord 1.15 p.m. Arrived Amiens 5.20 p.m. Left Blackett to go by train to 4th Army Inf. School, Flexicourt. Met Merriot and dinner with him at 'La Cathédral'. Met Kyle (Div. Padre) and Ford (Div. Battn's Officer) there. Slept at Hotel du Rhin.

Thursday 10th
Left Amiens about 10 a.m. and arrived at Roisel at 4 p.m. via 3 lorries, 2 cars and a considerable amount of walking. Big shells round about. Thunderstorm.

Friday 11th
Ordinary day – very hot.

Saturday 12th
Brig.-Gen. and Wallington to lunch.

Sunday 13th
Rifle Meeting in the afternoon. Saw St Quentin Cathedral (Bosch Land) from the high ground. Voluntary Church service in the open in the evening. Congregation somewhat disturbed during the sermon by seeing a fully inflated balloon being dragged along on the ground by about 40 men hanging on to the ropes. It looked

just like a huge caterpillar with the men as legs. Padre who came from a neighbouring Division (42nd?) stayed to dinner.

Monday 14th
Took A and B LG on range S of Roisel.

Tuesday 15th
2nd Cavalry Div. arrived and put horses and bivouacs all round our camp. Took C and D to range (LG) in afternoon.

Wednesday 16th
Left Roisel 12 noon by train for Merignolles. Had table and chairs in two horse-boxes for the officers. Much entertainment provided by one trench raiding the other at each half and carrying off persons and furniture (including whisky) as prisoners. A party of Bosch P. of W. at Chaunes looked on with amazement. Marched from Merignolles through Mericourt-s-Somme, where we passed the Major-Gen. in the rain, to old billet at Morcourt. Danny Mahor and Savin arrived.

Thursday 17th
McCabe went on leave. Met Angel who was now commanding No. 2 MG Coy.

Friday 18th
Rifle Meeting at 2.30 p.m. Old woman of an estaminet accused our men of stealing money. 3 Sgts were the accused. Went with a gendarme to search their billets.

Saturday 19th
Court of Enquiry re theft. Not sufficient evidence. Moved at 2.15 p.m. to Villers Bretonneux. Heard that I was to go on leave on Monday. Tea with Sheepshanks in a teashop. Clinton, who was commanding temporarily, gave me leave to go off at once. Hailed a Daimler and went to Amiens. Dinner at Savoy with Merriot who was still on sick leave.

Sunday 20th
Left Amiens at 12.16 a.m. Arrived Boulogne at 5.45 a.m. with Routledge RFC (the Douglas motorbike nephew). Breakfast at Officers' Club 6.15 a.m. Boat left at 8.15 a.m. Got as far as the gangway when the AMLO stopped everyone who was a day or more early. 'New order' he said. A colonel argued with him and failed, so I didn't bother to do ditto. Went to Wimereaux by train.

Lunched there, very bored. So returned and went to 2 cinemas. Dined at Mony, slept at the Louvre.

Monday 21st
Lunched at the Dervaux in La Grand Rue. [This was later on in the war completely destroyed by a bomb.] Went to cinema, met Hugh Barnes (Bde Intelligence Officer) and Lindsay and dined with them at the Folkestone.

Tuesday 22nd
Crossed on the SS *Victoria* about 10 a.m. Met Stroyan (Jesus, Cambridge) at Folkestone Harbour and Bruce Clark (Harrow) on the boat. Went to *Vanity Fair* at the Palace and met Abadie there.

Fourth Leave

June

Friday 1st
Left Victoria 8.05 a.m. Lunch at Metropole, Folkestone. Left 6 p.m. on Victoria (I think), arrived Boulogne 8 p.m. Dinner at Mony. Met Ritchie (RAMC) there. Slept at Hotel Dervaux.

Saturday 2nd
Tried to get on the ordinary train at 9.54 a.m. as the leave train started at 4 a.m. but was given a fatherly lecture by the RTO on obeying orders, ending up with a threat to report me to somebody or other for disobeying orders and extending my leave without permission. Amused myself by taking the train to Hardelot via Pont les Briques. Lunched at Hotel de l'Aviation and walked along the sea front. Bored, so trammed back to Boulogne and had dinner at Mony. Snoozed in armchair at the Officers' Club until it was time to go to the train about 2.30 a.m. (Sunday).

Sunday 3rd
Left Boulogne 4 a.m, arrived Bailleul about 11.30 a.m. Lunched at the Officers' Club. Jumped a lorry to Meteren. Vol. Service in a field in the evening. CO played 'Hullo My Dearie' and other and better tunes on the violin. Heberden accompanied him.

Monday 4th
Dinner with Chug Chambers (D Coy) who had arrived a few days before. All the Etonians went over to St Omer to feast and be merry.

Judging by the morrow, they were successful. Heard that Effie had got the Légion d'Honneur.

Tuesday 5th
CO and Forrest went to a lecture at Wisques.

Wednesday 6th
Glorious day and very hot. Route march to a canal in the Bois Clebent just S of Hazebrouck. Bathed and slept. Marched home in the evening. Rob got the MC.

Thursday 7th
Awakened about 4 a.m. by the trembling of the house caused by our huge mines being blown for the attack on the Messines Ridge.[10] Rehearsed singers for a concert in the YMCA hut. Col. Tolemache (NN) to dinner. Our band played. Thunderstorm.

Friday 8th
An ASCMT[11] officer to dinner.

Saturday 9th
Bde Rifle Meeting. Didn't go. Concert in YMCA hut at 8 p.m. Brig.-Gen. Hubbard was there. Rfm. Gee (a Battn tailor) gave an excellent ventriloquist turn.

Sunday 10th
Church parade, 9.10 a.m.

Monday 11th
Army didn't require our assistance so we moved at 8.12 a.m. to St Mairie Cappel near Cassel (army HQ) via Fletre, Caestre, and St Silvestre Cappel. Nice little bedroom on ground floor with flowers in the garden. Most of the villagers spoke Flemish which I heard for the first time. Bde HQ was in the village but the other battns were in neighbouring villages. A and D Coys were over a mile from Battn HQ.

Tuesday 12th
Walked with Gott and Hebenden to Cassel. Had an ice and explored the town. A most attractive old place right on the top of the only hill for miles. One was supposed to be able to see the sea from the Casino (Army HQ) terrace. Dawson went on leave, Butter's brother (from Army) to dinner.

Wednesday 13th
Run in early morning. Sat on FGCM.

Thursday 14th
FGCM sat for 5 minutes at 2 p.m. Dined on the terrace of the Hotel du Sauvage, Cassel, with Blackett and Chug. Good dinner and lovely view but an occasional doubtful smell from the back gardens below.

Friday 15th
Dined with Blackett at C Coy.

Saturday 16th
Marched to Forêt de Nieppe (part of which is the Bois Clebet where we went before), bathed and slept. Very hot and the canal was hot. Marched back through Hazebrouck. Delightful day but rather a long march.

Sunday 17th
Dinner with Fewtrell (orderly office at Bde) at Bde HQ BG and Wallington out to dinner. Met Padre Clayton (new Padre). Played bridge. Prosecuted at FGCM at 10 a.m.

Monday 18th
Bayonet fighting competition. Humphrey Butter went on leave so took over his job as usual. CO went to Boulogne in car to see him off and brought back some excellent soles.

Tuesday 19th
Cricket v 2nd Army Bomb School (away). Too busy to go. Blackett to dinner. The Mess Sgt. got a bathing costume for me at Hazebrouck as we heard we were going to the coast; and alarming orders had come round re officers not being allowed to bathe between certain spots, or hours, or both, unless in a 'regulation costume'. [This costume cost me Fr. 22.50 (worth 1/6d) and the only time it was ever used was in a pierrot show we gave at the beginning of July. Sheepshanks wore it as Chu Chin Chow (red and black latitudinal stripes).]

Wednesday 20th
Started in the cool of the morning (4.20 a.m.) for Wormhoudt. Arrived about 8 a.m. Rain. Had an excellent omelette with the CO at an hotel. Fielding (6th Battn Sheerness) to tea, also Forrest

who was away on a course of some sort at this time. Delightful billet over the mess.

Thursday 21st
Started at 3.40 a.m. for Rosendael (near Dunkerque), arrived about 9 a.m. Went by train to Dunkerque with the CO and Padre and had an omelette at Trassaert Frères. Dinner with Blackett, Chug, Chevis and Sheepers at the Ocean, Malo les Bains. It was a wonderful feeling being billeted with the whole Battn in a civilised town with big houses, trains and good shops.

Friday 22nd
Heard that we were to move on the following day but could get no definite order, so went to Bde HQ at Coudekerque Branche by train (changing at Dunkerque) to find out. They had no order there either. CO commander Bde and Lees (2nd in command) took over the Battn.

Belgium

Saturday 23rd
Moved at 5.30 a.m. and marched to station at Leffrinchoucke about a mile and a half. Train came at last at 7.30 a.m. Crossed the border and detrained on the line (no station) just beyond Coxyde at 10.45 a.m. Transport had gone by road but we had taken Coalbox in the train. Great difficulty and amusement in getting him out as there was no platform or ramp. Rigged up a sort of ramp with the wheeled stretcher covered with straw. By dint of pulling and pushing finally landed the little creature on his back in the sand (the railway was built on sand ballast). Marched through Coxyde Bains to Bador Camp on the dunes about 500 yards east. Div. HQ were billeted in various summer villas in Coxyde Bains. Duncan ADC to GOC Div. (Black Watch) who did the Div. HQ billeting, imbued with a sense of humour, put Jock Lloyd (the APM) in the 'Villa Tra-la-la'. All had strict orders to keep off the beach east of the Coxyde Road as it could be seen from Ostend. Sentries were posted at intervals along the dunes to keep people away.

Sunday 24th
Church at 9.45 a.m. in the theatre that the French had built in the Camp. Bathed in the sea (west of the aforesaid road). Padre to dinner.

Monday 25th
Calthorpe (Bde Major) and Dawson came back. Chug Chambers went to Australian Tunnelling Coy who were building tunnels in the dunes round about Nieuport Bains. Prosecuted at FGCM. Listened to Div. Band on the beach. CO and Col. Philips (LNL) to tea. A sentry of ours tried to arrest the Div. Padre for bathing east of the road. He was absolutely right and the Padre wrong.

Tuesday 26th
The Div. Concert Party (which had just come into being) took possession of our theatre. Heated argument between Lees and the OC Div. CP (Merifield SWB) about it as Blackett and I were getting up a pierrot show. However, Holbrook (AA & QMG) supported the Div. CP. Watched and criticised the show. Bathed. Shells landed on the beach and amongst the Munsters bathing party. A typical low Bosch trick! A sentry seeing Major-Gen. on the beach in the distance shouted to him to get off. Major-Gen. expostulated. When the sentry was asked afterwards if he didn't recognise the GOC by his 'Red' he said he thought it was a member of the MFP (Military Foot Police who sometimes wore a red crown to their hats).

Wednesday 27th
Posted patrols on the dunes instead of sentries. Rehearsed our concert in the evening. We had compromised with the DCP to rehearse when they were not using the theatre. The French came to take away their dynamo which had provided electric footlights etc. Very unfortunate.

Thursday 28th
Met Chug and Hunt (Bde Sig. Officer) at Field Cashier. Bought props and borrowed a pair of stays for the concert from a blushing maiden (about 40). Rehearsed in afternoon.

Friday 29th
Rehearsed with our band in afternoon. Doc Collier and Hunt to dinner. Concert at 8 p.m. in the Theatre. Pierrot troupe and skit jointly resembling *Chu Chin Chow* with the Hipperdrome touch of parading the auditorium.

Saturday 30th
Had photos taken of pierrot troupe in the open air. Windy. Tea at a cake shop with Blackett, Sheepers, Nigel Anson and Mills. Returned the stays. Rain.

July

Sunday 1st
Church Parade in the theatre 9.30 a.m. Rag rugger in the evening. Brig.-Gen. Hubbach, who had only just come back, and Calthorpe wounded. Yates shaken. Macarthy and his Adjt. (No. 2 FA) wounded. Humphrey came back.

Monday 2nd
Went to see the plates of the photos.

Tuesday 3rd
Moved to Rinck camp just west of Ouest-Dunkerque-Bains with 'Details'. ['Details' were the nucleus of the Battn that was always to be left out of the line when the Battn went into any line. It was then quite a new idea but proved very useful within the next few days]. The remainder of the Battn moved to Nieuport Bains to take over Support Area. We turned out the band to play the Battn by as they went up.

Wednesday 4th
Battn moved up to extreme left sector of the whole western front (Lombartzyde area). The left sentry was actually on the beach. While in the Béthune area we had often thought how weird it would be to be on the extreme left or right (Switzerland) of the Front. As usual when we took over from a peaceful French Front it became violent within a few days. Rob went on leave. Chug came back to Details from the Tunnelling Coy. Tea in Coxyde-Bains with Blackett. Explored Ouest-Dunkerque-Bains after tea.

Thursday 5th
Saw photos of pierrot troupe, bathed and tea at Coxyde-Bains. Dinner at 2nd Bde HQ. During this past fortnight there were shoals of jellyfish and hundreds of men were stung. Some even went to hospital for a few days. We used to shriek and run (or swim) for our lives whenever we saw one.

Friday 6th
Bathed. Nigel Anson slightly wounded so came back to Details and Golding went up to take his place. Brig.-Gen. Kemp CB (RE) took over the Bde and Abadie took over the Battn in the line. Lees came down and went on leave.

Saturday 7th
Quiet day.

Sunday 8th
Church Parade in 1st Div. Canteen Hut. Fetched photos of pierrot troupe. Nigel took them up the line as he had recovered, and Golding came back again.

Monday 9th
Rhodesians under McDowell did a raid. McDowell wounded. Warner came down and Heberden went up in his place. I went up to Nieuport Bains by tunnel to arrange relief for the next day. The Battn was to be relieved by the 1st LNL who were then in Nieuport Bains and to take over their cellars. Heberden was killed and also Smith (Northants) attached to TMB.

Tuesday 10th
Bosch started strafing about 6 a.m. Plastered every square yard of ground from our front line back to behind Coxyde. Every sort of gun was used. Even we in the Details had 5 killed. All the base lines round about suffered many casualties. We knew something was up, but could get no definite news. A terrible day for us but infinitely worse for the Battn in flimsy dug-outs built in the sand. At last 8.30 p.m. arrived and I took up the billeting party (5 or 6 NCO's) according to orders. I avoided the road, beach and tunnel and dodged about the dunes up to LNL HQ. I arrived panting and was greeted by LNL Intelligence Officer with 'Hallo, haven't you heard? Your Battn has been scuppered.'
[The Bosch had attacked at 7.15 p.m. by which time most of the Battn and the Northants on our right had been killed or buried in the dug-outs or sand. A company cook in a cookhouse had told Battn HQ that a party of Bosch were coming round from the beach in rear. They entered one end of a tunnel into which Battn HQ had moved, so HQ moved along to the other end, but there was such a crowd of Tunnellers and others that they got disconnected from the CO who was never seen again. Rfm. Smart, an orderly, put old tins in the way behind him and the Bosch were heard swearing and tumbling over them as they came along. We shall never know the heroic deeds of Riflemen on that day. Tony Clinton's company evidently put up a gallant fight as the Bosch were seen to hesitate in that area. Gott volunteered time after time to go up to the front line to get news for the CO. The air, and even streets of Nieuport Bains were thick with Bosch planes but none of ours were seen. None of our big guns which were being brought up into that area fired a shot. The Div. Artillery fired all they knew but of course were useless against the gigantic preparations of the Bosch. A Bosch officer afterwards told Doc Ward who was taken prisoner that they

had concentrated 83 *extra* batteries of 4 or 6 guns each on to the two Battn fronts. They used picked Marines for the job. They were completely successful and captured all the ground (about 600-yards deep) up to the Yser Canal, thus preventing our troops from having 600 yards of land to jump off from in the forthcoming offensive.]

The only communication existing between the east of the Canal and our main territory west of it was 3 wooden footbridges. These, of course, were demolished by noon.

After seeing that I could do nothing at the LNL HQ and moreover appeared to be in the way, I collected all my party that I could find and started for home. Before I'd got out of the tunnel I ran into a party of M. Gunners coming up. They were sitting on the floor coughing and spitting. A shell had just dropped into the tunnel and they said it was the fumes. A very young officer was in charge. I sniffed and said it was a gas shell. The MGs, however, said it wasn't and remained sitting in the middle of it. I told my party to put on their masks and we got out of the tunnel through the hole made by the shell. I couldn't help thinking of the White Rabbit in *Alice in Wonderland* running along the passage saying 'I shall be late' and bumping into Alice who had just eaten the cake that made her grow. (Whether the MGs ever found out whether it was gas before it was too late I never knew.)

We then continued our hectic walk, or half run, partly along the beach and partly along the dunes and eventually got back to Rinck Camp.

Wednesday 11th
Effie, Humphrey and Gracie (Sig. Off.) arrived back about 2 a.m. frozen. They, with about 15 men (but all independently) had swum the canal in the dark and had been given whisky by the LNL. We each looked after one person, I looking after Effie, taking off his clothes and tucking him up in my bed.

Thursday 12th
About 25 more men, mostly of B Coy, got back by swimming the Canal. They had been buried and had dug themselves out during the day. They were all prepared to give themselves up to the Bosch but seeing none they made their way to the Canal. It appeared that the Bosch, very wisely, only had sentries on the captured ground by night and left it alone during the day. Charles Blowet RFC (Harrow) came to lunch with Humphrey. Went to Corps Main Dressing Station to try and find out something about some of the missing. Brig.-Gen. Kemp

addressed the remains of the Battn at 5.30 p.m. and struck the right note.

The following is the officers' casualty list for 10th July. Missing and presumed dead: Col. Abadie, Sheepshanks, Barnes (Rhodesian), Munroe (Rhodesian), Anson, Boucher. The following were Prisoners of War: Doc Ward, Gott, Taylor, Clinton, Simpson, Mills, Chevis, Pinnoch, Madeley, Lindsay. [We only knew that the first three were prisoners at once; the other names coming through later.] Col. Tolemache (Northants) was also captured. Pallant, MO of the LNL did excellent work getting ropes across the river to help our men who couldn't swim.

Friday 13th
Major-Gen. Strickland spoke to the two Battns at 12 noon. He, as always, said just the right thing. Humphrey went to GHQ to be interviewed by Sir Douglas Haig. Spent a busy day with papers etc. Got the wind up in the evening.

Saturday 14th
Mason and Webster (new Doc) arrived. Busy day in the Orderly Room. Gracie and 7 other 'swimmers' went on special leave. Effie commanded the Battn.

France

Sunday 15th
Moved at 9.45 a.m. to Ghyvelde through Coxyde and Adinkerk, arrived about 2.30 p.m. Tents with a house for HQ officers. We moved in the 3rd Bde group as the 2nd Bde were still holding the line for a day or two. Received orders to move next day in the middle of the night.

Monday 16th
Moved 7.15 a.m. to Capelle a few miles south of Dunkerque. Arrived about 12.30 p.m. Lt.-Gen. Du Cane GOC XV Corps, spoke to officers of Northants and ourselves. A most unfortunate speech and very different from our Brigadier and Divisional Commander. His theme was that we were not in any way to blame. None of us had any intention of blaming ourselves. Battn then marched past him in column of route. Marched through Uxem and Boomkems. Draft of good keen men, but with no knowledge of infantry work, arrived about 10 p.m. There were 236 of them, a good many from ASC. Much business in billeting them in the school.

Tuesday 17th
Elsie Barnes rejoined and Rob and Hill came back from leave.
They all drove up in a station fly, which looked odd somehow.
Draft of 161 other ranks arrived about 6 p.m. Still more difficulty
about billeting them and rationing them. Humphrey came back
from GHQ.

Wednesday 18th
Heard that we were to move to Le Clipon on the coast into a sort of
Hush Camp. We had every wagon loaded and horses in when the
move was cancelled. We were still under the 3rd Bde and orders
took rather a long time coming via them and then on to us. Went to
Chug's billet and talked to the lady of the house who was Scotch.

Thursday 19th
Did the billeting at St Pol near Dunkerque with the CQMSs.
The men and some officers in tents on the dunes. HQ mess in
a farmhouse. Battn arrived about 5 p.m. CJ Read arrived. Slept
with Humphrey in an estaminet. Under 2nd Brigade again.

Friday 20th
A Bombing and Lewis Gun instructor (one of each) arrived from
the Div. School to help us train the new drafts.

Saturday 21st
Babe Buckland, Cook (New Army), Cummin (an elderly gentle-
man) and Braybrooke arrived. Lt.-Col. Willan arrived to take over
the Battn. Effie went on leave.

Sunday 22nd
Bde Church Parade on the dunes. Major Bryce (New Army) and
Ormrod arrived. Eddie Campbell went on leave. After the smash
the higher authorities asked us what sort of officers were required.
We replied saying subalterns. They therefore included one Major
and two Captains.

Monday 23rd
CO went away to a conference. Had a delightful bathe in salt water
moat round Fort Mardick. Deep and warm and no jellyfish.

Tuesday 24th
Col. Willan's brother (2nd Army Signals) and Fladgate (2nd Army
Signals and Harrow) came to see us. Major Burt (113 Battery RFA)
also came. Miss Grant and a man from the YMCA came to see me

re getting men to perform at YMCA concerts. Gave them tea at HQ. Bathed in the moat. Watched the Div. Concert Party at the Northants. CO returned.

Wednesday 25th
Bathed in moat. Saw the 'Chinks' (Chinese Labour Corps) returning from the beach. They picked up jellyfish from the sands and ate them on the spot which seemed to me somewhat strange. Willmott, Shaw and Harmon arrived.

Thursday 26th
Bathed in moat. Bryce left.

Friday 27th
Tea with Miss Grant in YMCA hut at St Pol. Dinner with D Coy.

Saturday 28th
Bde Horse Show and Vehicle Competition 2 p.m. Bathed in the moat 5.30 p.m. and found that the RAMC had put up a diving board. Fired LG into the sea in morning.

Sunday 29th
Paraded for Church Parade but cancelled owing to rain. Bury and CO's brother came over. Grundy arrived. Dined with Elsie (A Coy).

Monday 30th
Wet in the morning. Moved at 2.20 p.m. to the Hush Camp at Le Clipon. All tents with two Nissen huts for messes. Drizzle in evening.
[The whole Division was interned in this camp to train for landing from Monitors round about Ostend. The QM Stores and all Div. Transport were outside the camp and no intercourse was allowed between those inside and those out. Anyone could come in, but once in they had to stay in. Field ambulances were in so however ill a person became he still remained in. All officers' letters were to be censored by the CO. There was a 60-centimetre railway to take rations etc. from the gates to the various units. The gates were in the form of a river lock. That is the outside people brought rations etc. into the lock and the inside people took them over. There were MFP there to see that the inside held no conversation in private with the outside. Battn were allowed out for route marches etc., but no individuals were to attempt to get out on pain of instant death (if the Sentries' aim were good). It

was all very interesting and one really began to feel that we were at last getting on with the War.]

Tuesday 31st[12]
Rain all day. The one great advantage of living on dunes was that there was never any mud, however much it rained.

August

Wednesday 1st
Rain all day. Sgt. Hoare (Band Sgt.) arrived.

Thursday 2nd
Band played in the evening and also for Bde Mess. Played soccer HQ v A Coy on the sand. Very boring. HQ won 2–1. Rain on and off all day. Readdie to dinner with D Coy. Rag in the evening.

[These rags occurred fairly often and consisted amongst other things of running up other people's tents when they were in bed and then letting them down on top of the sleepers. I had a pair of black and white striped pyjamas which was excellent camouflage at night, rendering me quite invisible at a few yards distance.]

Friday 3rd
Rain on and off all day. Faman arrived back.

Saturday 4th
Route March through Loon Plage. No rain and the band played well.

Sunday 5th
Sun shone all day. Bde Church parade 10.30 a.m. 25th Bde RFA attended as well. We had sent on an orderly to find the way and when he was guiding us he lost himself. We eventually spotted the entire congregation assembled waiting for us (our band was to play the service). We thereupon took a straight cut leaping over fences and ditches and arrived in extended order through the Sussex cookhouses. It must have looked most impressive. Bishop of Khartoum presided from the top of a pile of full SAA boxes. Bathed in the afternoon (direct from our sleeping tent) and afterwards played catch ball dashing about the sands in nature's dress. The feeling that one could roam about naked without shocking anybody was delightful.

We raided the TMB and MGC after dinner. Great fun. We unhooked the MGC's limbers and moved them about. Angel (OC

2nd MGC) came out and started putting sentries under arrest for not shooting. We were all in hiding amongst the little furze bushes and heard him give orders to shoot. Whereupon the sentry rattled his bolt in a most alarming manner. We eventually captured most of the officers and brought them back to our mess. (It took 6 of us to carry Readdie). We then filled them with whisky. It all ended happily and they promised to raid us on a future occasion.

Monday 6th
CSM Hawker (Rifle Bde) an instructor from GHQ school arrived to help train LGs. He toured the various Battns staying 4 days with each. Played rounders.

Tuesday 7th
Hectic walk through rifle barrage to the western boundary of the Camp with Cheyney. Whenever anybody wanted to do a realistic scheme they took the sea for the enemy and fired live rounds by the hundred into it. Anybody walking along the beach was therefore apt to be potted.

Wednesday 8th
Played rounders.

Thursday 9th
Bathed. Tea with 2nd Bde HQ.

Friday 10th
Nugent Head, Cheyney, Gurney, Johnson, Winter, Palmer, Trinder, White, Hancock arrived. The first three were regulars, the rest temporary. Raid by MGC and TMB. Humphrey of course finished up by bleeding. He always seemed to get damaged. Band played at Mess. Our pipers whom Abadie had introduced also played. Battn played Sussex at soccer. We won 5–2.

Saturday 11th
The whole of the 2nd Bde rehearsed the landing from a dummy pontoon on land. All the vehicles and little hand-carts were there and the whole proceedings were timed. Saw the RQMS in fighting order for the first time. He was to have been in charge of rations etc. on the sea journey and was therefore in the camp. The QM on the other hand was to be in charge of rations coming up by road with the transport, after the attacking troops from Nieuport etc. had pushed the Bosch back (eastwards). Watched the Div. Concert Party in the evening.

Sunday 12th
Bde Church Parade 10 a.m. Practised climbing the sea wall at 12.30 p.m. This was a huge concrete wall about 45° slope with one half of the top straight and the other half forming a concave facing you as you toiled up. This afforded much amusement. Some people made a dash for it and stuck after about 6 paces, others took it gently and stuck after about 15 paces. Success lay in keeping your whole weight forward and walking on the toes. The stretcher bearers and Lewis Gunners carrying their long narrow-shaped burdens seemed to find less difficulty. There were sort of baskets at the top of the wall which, when hurled down the slope at carefully balanced individuals, entirely carried their feet away. They then slowly slid down feet first on their chests. (This latter obstacle was only used against officers after the serious part of the entertainment was over). The top of the wall was roughly 20ft high and was built against a higher level of dunes so that one could walk away on the level when one had gained the summit. The whole was carefully camouflaged and had sentries round it night and day. The idea of the wall was that there might be one opposite the actual spot where we should land. I was told that tanks were to have special grappling irons and were to haul up guns, ambulances, motor-cycles and side-cars and all manner of vehicles.

Bathed, but too many jellyfish so came out quickly. Effie came back. Bde hired a piano for the use of the Battns. We had first use and it arrived in the afternoon.

Monday 13th
Route march through Mardick, Grande-Synthe, Petite-Synthe and Fort Mardick. Effie became gastronomic Mess President and I became financial Mess President. Went through the books with Lees and found that absolutely no check had been kept over the Mess Sgt.'s accounts. Now he was outside the Camp and I was in. I tried sending him notes duly censored but he took very little notice of them. So I arranged an appointment at the Lock where we stood one each side of the gate discussing matters with several MFPs around. Bathed, still many jellyfish. Walked along the beach after dinner with Blackett and Elsie watching the phosphorescent waves. One or two enthusiasts used to bathe by night and they looked very weird with their bodies glowing with the phosphorus.

Tuesday 14th
Paddled before breakfast (don't know why). Lots of jellyfish. Prosecuted at FGCM. Sorted library books that had arrived from Padre for use of the men. Songs and piano after dinner.

Wednesday 15th
Rehearsed for small concert at 2.30 p.m. Cull went to TMB. Boxing competition. Rfm McMahon won the welter-weight.

Thursday 16th
Field Day with live shells etc. 12 noon–4 p.m. Brig.-Gen. Kemp to dinner. Concert in Church Army Tent 8 p.m. Dined in C and D Mess (HQ A and B formed the other mess). Readdie was there.

Friday 17th
Michael Wallington to dinner. Sang and piano after. Bathed. Soccer match 6-a-side. Battn HQ v Bde HQ Officers.

Saturday 18th
Bathed in big waves. Platoon competition over an obstacle course that had been put up. Sussex won. Played rounders. Sang and piano after dinner.

Sunday 19th
Bde Church Parade in morning. Lovely afternoon. Bathed. Effie danced pas seul in state of nudity except a loin cloth (towel). Very graceful. Our band was playing suitable minuets and gavottes. Soccer v Bde. We won 4–0.

Monday 20th
Rugger practice on the sands. Bathed and played about with a rowing boat. The Sussex were trying to carry out field firing into the sea, but our boat got in the way. Lovely afternoon. Babe Bucklands's 21st dinner. Much noise and some damage.

Tuesday 21st
Rugger v Northants. We won 47–4. Watched Div. Concert Party. Companies made rafts of canvas and brushwood.

Wednesday 22nd
Soccer v Sussex. 2 all. Bathed with jellyfish. [We had got large fishing nets and companies used to go out with them dragging the sea. They caught many fish and on more than one occasion caught enough to provide the whole Coy with fish for breakfast.]

Thursday 23rd
Col. Phillips LNL, Jock Lloyd, Backhouse (2nd in Command Northants) to dinner and small concert in Church Army Tent afterwards. I sang 'My Friend John' with difficulty.

Friday 24th
The whole Division rehearsed for an inspection on the beach in the morning. Effie and I watched from the dunes. Showers of rain. Bathed in rough sea with much wind. Humphrey's horse wouldn't keep still and caused much language from Major-General during the rehearsal.

Saturday 25th
General Rawlinson GOC 4th Army inspected the complete Division, RAMC, MMG, ASC etc., drawn up in line on the beach. A wonderful sight. We all marched past, (Coys in line). I took Adjt.'s part as Humphrey was to receive his bar to MC after the march past. Was very nervous about my horse, whether it would do what Humphrey's did on the day before. However, it (The Rabbit) stood perfectly still. Played rounders.

Sunday 26th
Church Parade on beach with Northants. Rugger v Sussex. We won 37–0. We were champions of 2nd Bde thanks mainly to Gracie, Chug Chambers and Elsie.

[About this time we heard that the landing would not come off as the attacks on the high ground (Passchendaele Ridge) overlooking the coast had failed. Some of the more stringent orders were now relaxed, but we were still to treat the whole matter as secret.]

Monday 27th
Rain. Called in Lindsell (Adjt. LNL) to arrange about the piano coming back. Went to the cinema that had now been erected in an old aeroplane hanger, one of the rope and canvas variety. Rain came through the roof and a very bad show.

Tuesday 28th
Rain and wind all day. Everybody busy with their tents. Both the Church Army Tent and Cinema were flattened out.

Wednesday 29th
Route march in rain storm. Rounders in evening, Bde and Battn HQ v Rest of Battn.

Thursday 30th
Rain.

Friday 31st
A and B Coys formed the enemy to a Bde attack. Some sailors from the Monitors that were to have helped us in the landing arrived as guests of Div. The Monitors were anchored just off the coast.

September

Saturday 1st
2nd Bde Soccer semi-final v Sussex. 2 all. Gracie broke a small bone in his hand.

[This was full moon and we were to hear the Bosch planes bombing Dunkerque and Calais on each side of us. We also heard them flying over to England. They never hit our camp although some 'archies' fell near the Transport outside.]

Sunday 2nd
Bde Church Parade on the beach.

Monday 4th
Elsie went on leave.

Tuesday 5th
Soccer semi-final. We replayed Sussex and won 1–0. Humphrey and Michael went on leave. Bathed, rather cold.

Wednesday 6th
Field Day with Sappers, Cyclists and MMGs. Bathed.

Thursday 7th
Col. Willan left to take over the 56th Inf Bde Moved the position of C and D's Nissen hut.

Friday 8th
Battn acted as enemy to 2nd Bde. Moved off at 6.15 a.m, returned at 4.15 p.m.

Saturday 9th
Soccer final v LNL. We lost 0–3.

Sunday 10th
Church Parade on the beach 10.30 a.m. Bathed in the afternoon. Col. Kelly arrived to command the Battn. Was introduced to him with only a towel round me.

Monday 10th
Ordinary day. Rehearsed pierrot troupe.

Tuesday 11th
Watched a demonstration of Message Carrying rockets. More sailors arrived. Some of them were off to tour the Messines Battlefields in lorries. Tug of war v MGC. We won. Concert with pierrot troupe in Cinema at 8.30 p.m.

Wednesday 12th
Kelly startled to find that the person who claimed to be his Adjt. was clean-shaven, whereas the person to whom he was introduced on Sunday had a moustache. (Solution: I had shaved for the part of Pierrette). Sailors returned from Messines. Tug of War semi-final v Northants. We won. Pull lasted 6 minutes. Elsie returned.

Thursday 13th
Hectic changes re orders for sailors. Too rough to put out to Monitors, so they went by lorry at 1.45 p.m. to Dunkerque and got on board that way. Tug of War final v Sussex. We lost. Our pierrot troupe performed at Northants Concert in cinema.

Wednesday 14th
Blackett and I went in Constable's (Bde Major) Ford car to Boulogne. He was going on leave and we were again going to Paris. Left in the dark at 4.30 a.m. We left Boulogne at 2.15 p.m, arrived Paris 8.20 p.m. Met a very pleasant French civilian in the train who insisted on showing us the way from the Gare du Nord by metro to the Rue de Rivoli and then back to Hotel d'Edouard VII. He warned us very gravely about the evils of Paris.

Saturday 15th
Lunch at Boeuf à la Mode. Dinner with Effie and his sister at Café de Paris. Saw Regine Flory at the Vaudeville. (We also saw her at the Edouard VII the next day.)

Sunday 16th
Lunch at Laperouse. Dinner at a grill room. Opera Comique *Carmen*.

Monday 17th
Lunch at Boeuf à la Mode. Went to Luxembourg Gardens. Dinner at La Rue. Tea at Rumplemeyers. Femina 'Sappho'.

Tuesday 18th
Lunch at Ambassadeurs. Car to Chantilly. Dinner at La Rue. Saw Spinelli in the original French revue *As You Were* at the Michael. We were in the front row and the only 'orchestra' was a very old man at the piano. He sat right between my legs.

Wednesday 19th
Lunch at Café de Paris. Dinner also there where we met the Babe and Ormrod. Follies Bergère.

Thursday 20th
Lunch at La Rue. Car to St Germain. Axle broke. Ormrod, Blackett and I came back by tram leaving the Babe with the car. Blackett and I had dinner at the Gare du Nord and left at 7.20 p.m.

Friday 21st
Arrived Calais at 8.15 a.m. Took Winnie to lunch at the Continental. Left 5.23 p.m. and arrived Loon Plage Station at 6.45 p.m. Arrived at the Camp about 8.15 p.m.

Saturday 22nd
Quiet day. Most of the officers went on a staff ride in buses. Humphrey and I carried out Battn drill on the sands.

Sunday 23rd
2nd Bde Race Meeting on the sands. Jockeys weighed by Rob on his meat-weighing machine. 3 bands played. The Regiment got one 1st a 2nd, and a 3rd.

Monday 24th
Practice rugger v SWB on their ground (grass not sand). 5.30 p.m. We lost 0–8. Bathed, very calm. Cloudless day.

Tuesday 25th
Field Day at Mardick. I was a sort of Umpire. Bathed. Very warm. Cloudless day.

Wednesday 26th
Dull day. Practice rugger on the sands. 2nd Lt. HJ Fletcher, 1st Wilts Yeomanry (disbanded) joined as Transport Officer.
[He carried out Riding Classes for Yeomanry Officers on the beach in the evenings. Most amusing. Some horses climbed the steepest dunes with their riders clinging on to their necks. Others deposited their burdens on the sand, and others would suddenly

roll without giving notice to the unfortunate individual who did think he was safe when the horse was standing still. Humphrey often taken as Squadron Leader in Cavalry Drill.]

Thursday 27th
Bde Field Day which I got out of owing to LG classes. Bathed in the evening.

Friday 28th
Quiet day. Michael to dinner.

Saturday 29th
Attended Michael's farewell dinner. He was going to 1st Bde as Bde Major. Very cheery and certain amount of damage to Bde crockery. Chichester Constable (Bde Major) and others performed the feat of climbing through the roof window in the canvas lining of the marquee, and sliding down the said lining and appearing under the curtains. Noise on the piano. Lost my shirt. During the afternoon the Battn practised boarding and arranging themselves on an imitation Monitor (i.e., a grass space with the turf removed to represent funnels etc.)

Sunday 30th
Bde Church Parade 10 a.m. on the beach. Lecture by Maj.-Gen. Montgomery[13] on the war at 2.30 p.m. Laurence, Michael, Eddie and 'Chic' (Bde Major) to dinner. Bathed.

October

Monday 1st
Div. Rugger semi-final v 1st Gloucesters (3rd Bde). We lost 0–13.

Tuesday 2nd
Field Day round Pte. Synthe and Moulin Spycker. Div. informed me that I was a full Lt. as from 1st July 1917. Bathed.

Wednesday 3rd
Watched demonstration of SOS Red smoke daylight signal. Windy day. Weather probably broken. Cherry went on leave. Cross-country race. We were 4th.

Thursday 4th
Played bridge in the afternoon. Discovered deficiencies in Mess a/cs which were made up to 30th Sept. Took LGs night firing into the sea. Used the luminous sights.

Friday 5th
Went to Calais in ambulance to get big drum skin and whisky.
Stubbs (RAMC) was going in so I got a lift. Took Winnie to lunch
at Continental.

Saturday 6th
Wet.

Sunday 7th
Wet. Court of enquiry on Mess a/cs.

Monday 8th
Started new LG course.

Tuesday 9th
Bde Field Day round about Fort Mardyck. Mason's 21st Birthday
dinner. Usual developments.

Wednesday 10th
Walked to No. 1 FA with Warner in the evening.

Thursday 11th
Went in MMG car to Dunkerque to interview the Bank and EFC[14]
about cheques re Mess a/cs. Had lunch at the Arcades. Tea with
MMG (14th Battery). Lecture by Captain Smythe (4th Army) on
aeroplane photos.

Friday 12th
Gen. Rawlinson talked to us in the cinema at 2.15 p.m. Told us
that the landing would not come off this year, but it might the
next, so it was still secret. Half C Coy did a stunt for Rawly and
Neville Chamberlain[15] afterwards.

Saturday 13th
Wet all day. Dined with Northants and did pierrot show for them
at their concert.

Sunday 14th
Major-General inspected drafts. Brig.-Gen. presented Rfm Bradley
with Royal Humane Society's parchment. Faman went on leave to
Dieppe. Head and others went on leave to Paris.

Monday 15th
Gracie's 21st birthday. Usual celebrations. Hubbard joined the
Battn as an officer (Rhodesian).

Tuesday 16th
Cherry returned. Cavalry drill on the beach.

Wednesday 17th
Practised a special show for Americans.

Thursday 18th
Carried out demonstration of modern attack for the benefit of the higher American command. On seeing our men lying in extended order in a muddy field one American was heard to say 'Very fine, but where is the rear rank?' I did a sort of ADC's job looking after Red Hats. Brig.-Gen. Serocold (OC 2nd Battn in 1914) came to lunch. Brig.-Gen. Ready left the 1st Bde.

Friday 19th
Lt.-Col. Clarke XV Corps MG officer lectured to us in the afternoon. Angel and his MGs demonstrated overhead barrage into the sea. We were all assembled in front of the MGs and watched the bullets hitting the water. Angel walked along the edge of the sea to show us how accurate were his calculations.

Saturday 20th
Another MG barrage along the beach. Did a small pierrot show at a concert in the cinema at 8.30 p.m.

Sunday 21st
Got orders to move next day. Humphrey lunched and dined out so left me to cope with Battn orders. It was surprising how difficult it was to move after being in one spot for 3 months. All the QM branch said the accumulation of baggage was too much for them. First of all it had to be loaded on the 60cm railway and then loaded on lorries and GS wagons and limbers at the lock gates.

Monday 22nd
Superintended the loading. One truck came off the line and deposited all its load at the junction thus blocking the line in both directions. Moved at 8.15 a.m, lunched in a field and arrived round about Eringhem, west of Wormhoudt at 4.45 p.m. HQ Mess in a farm. Slept in tents. All 4 scattered miles away.

Tuesday 23rd
Wet and *mud* again. After orders for move the next day had gone out, Effie and I were sent to 2 Coys each to see if they understood them. I rode the only available bicycle in the moonlight to A and

C. A were playing cards and gave me a drink. C were all in bed and cursed me for waking them up. Rode back and reported 'all understood, sir'.

Wednesday 24th
Left at 8 a.m. for near Nouveau Monde between Wormhoudt and Herzeele. Marched through Esquelbecq. Arrived 1 p.m. Blackett twisted his ankle and had to ride on a lorry.

Belgium

Thursday 25th
Left at 8.20 a.m, for Schools Camp west of Poperinghe, via Houtkerque and Watou. McCabe went on leave. Golding returned. Passed lot of shanties built by refugees from Ypres etc. These shanties were made of British biscuit tins and all sorts of odd bits of wood. Arrived about 12 noon.

Friday 26th
The Mess was a Hospital Nissen hut with empty windows. Slept in Nissen hut. The men slept in bell tents that were sunk into the ground about a foot and had sand bags built round about 2ft high. Transport lines were likewise protected. This was because of the new Bosch bombs which had what corresponded to our 106 fuse and which went off the instant they touched and scattered their fragments horizontally. Very uncomfortable and wet all day. Sneddon rejoined.

Saturday 27th
Jumped lorry to Poperinghe. Left the Station about 11 a.m. Arrived Boulogne 7.50 p.m. Dinner at Mony. Slept at Hotel de Paris.

Sunday 28th
Left in the morning on SS *Victoria*, arrived Victoria 3.30 p.m.

Fifth Leave

November

Wednesday 7th[16]
Left Victoria 8.15 a.m. 'all change' at Shorncliffe. Told to conduct troops to the camp, but retired to the lavatory and when all was clear came out disguised by having removed my British Warm[17]. Went on to Folkestone by ordinary train. Lunch at the Grand. Left

Folkestone at 4 p.m. While on the boat a man again collared me for duty and as security took away my warrant, telling me to report at No. 6 cabin a quarter of an hour before the boat arrived. This was a card in my hand as I didn't know when the boat would arrive until it arrived. Trouble at the gangway as I hadn't got my warrant, so was told by the SM to 'wait over there'. As that was only about 2 yards away and in a strong light I did so. Various blue hats approached and finally told me to go and report at the head of the column of troops waiting to toil up the hill to the camp. Thought it advisable to find out when my train left so first went to the station and discovered it left at 12.50 that night. By the time I had deposited my pack in the cloakroom, somehow or other the column had gone. Dined at Mony, and went on to the Station afterwards.

Thursday 8th
Left Boulogne at 12.50 a.m. and arrived Poperinghe about 9.30 a.m. Nobody seemed to know where the Div. was and the Div. rest camp NCO said he was expecting a new location list at any minute. Met Brady and lunched with him at the officers' club. Went to a Div. Show *The Goods*. Slept at the Club.

Friday 9th
Got lift to just east of Vlamertinghe. Wandered through miles of various divisions' transport on mud and sleeper roads. Nobody had ever heard of the 1st Division. Heard a shell and saw the burst for the first time since July. Didn't like it. It was a quick one. At last spotted our divisional sign (blue pennant with white edge and white circle in the middle) on a GS wagon and jumped with joy.

Found Rob and Effie in a Nissen hut in a sea of mud at Reigersburg Camp near Brielan (SE of it). Heard that the Battn was in the line and were coming out that night. Bristowe came to see us. Went up in the evening with Effie to Irish Farm and Hill Top Farm to wait for the Battn and receive them. These two camps were on high ground between St Jean and Pilkem. The whole area was mud, dumps and guns. No one single tree, bush or blade of grass or house, of course, was visible; and these camps consisting of unlined Nissen huts stood out and were visible for miles around (including the eastern direction). Waited till 11 p.m. and then came home to the QM stores at Reigersburg.

Saturday 10th
Rain. Went up to Hill Top in the morning to arrange Battn. Willan (Brig.-Gen.) came to see us at QM Stores. Went up again to Hill Top in afternoon to relieve Humphrey.

106

Sunday 11th

Relieved Northants at the Paddebeke (a little stream). Started in single file at 3.15 p.m. and walked from the St Julien soup kitchen along rails of duck-board raised well off the surface of the mud. If a Rfm. had fallen off when carrying full kit he probably would never have got on again alone. I always hated the actual moving into the line, but I think I hated this one the most. It seemed never ending and there wasn't a single landmark. Occasionally a shell had hit the duck-boards and one had to wade round the edge of the hole and then find the track again the other side. However, we finally broke away from the track and made for a pill box with a few stumps of trees nearby. This was Battn HQ and just held the CO, myself and two signallers. The remainder of the HQ staff, a couple or orderlies, one servant and the Provost Sgt., and perhaps one other lived in a 'lean-to'. The floor of the pill box was a foot or more mud and water and a trench-board was fixed just above. If one dropped a pencil or a watch, it was gone for ever.

[Some months later an enterprising HQ cleaned the whole place out and it was not till then that the bottom was discovered.] The relief was completed about 9 p.m. [This pill box was afterwards known as Burns Houses.]

Monday 12th

No rain and fairly quiet. Padre Clayton came up and I took him to B Coy. This was a dreadful journey as no track went there. Rfm. Proctor, a Rhodesian, and by no means young, had a wonderful knack of finding his way. He used to put his head on the ground and take his bearings in a manner that filled me, a Londoner, with admiration. I couldn't see anything to take bearings on.

[I must state that all movement was by night; only an occasional urgent message being sent by runner during the day. The men, poor souls, lived in shell-holes and had hot food and tea brought up to them at night; Sgt. Whittington of the Band was indefatigable in conducting carrying parties at all hours of the night. Each Battn only spent 48 hours in the front line in these parts].

[Padre Clayton used to live at the St Julian Soup Kitchen and night after night would come right up to the front posts with cigarettes etc. for the men. He always went alone, knowing perfectly well that if a bullet caught him he'd roll off the duck-board into the mud and stay there. Occasionally he would tack himself on to a relief or carrying party and then would insist on carrying someone's load. He afterwards got the MC for this work. There was no continuous line now – only isolated posts of a section or platoon. It sometimes happened that a Coy Commander would be unable to see one of his posts during the 48 hours. On one occasion the CO spent the whole of one night looking for a Coy HQ and came back at dawn without having found it. You not only had to find what you were looking for, but you had to avoid finding a Bosch post. No-one knew where the Bosch were: and beyond the fact that the Bosch knew where their own pill boxes were, that they had built and we had captured, they didn't know where we were.]

Tuesday 13th
Relieved by Northants. Came out via Hubner Farm – a large pill box with several partitions and inhabited by Gunners. Stopped at the Soup Kitchen and had some delicious soup. Went back to Hill Top. Blackett hit in the thigh.

Wednesday 14th
Moved back to Dambre Camp between Vlamertinghe and Elverdinghe. Met Hackworth (Jesus).

Thursday 15th
Had a bath in another Division's baths. Shelled more or less in the evening with HV guns.

Friday 16th
HV guns shelled us about 5.30 p.m. Most alarming as there was absolutely no cover. Several casualties in the other units, but none in the Battn.

Saturday 17th
Shelled at 8 p.m. when Cockson, our mess waiter, was hurled into the Mess scattering his tray, and again at midnight. Very unpleasant as one lay in a flea bag in an unprotected Nissen hut. Doc Madill (who had taken the place of Webster at Le Clipon), an Irishman, sought to soothe us by reading Omar Khayyam.

Sunday 18th
Moved at 1.30 p.m. to Reigersburg Camp with the details. The Battn moved up to Irish Farm where they were bombed in broad daylight. We were shelled just as we moved off from Dambre Camp.

Monday 19th
Forrest came to tea. Took soup party up as far as St Julien Dump and returned home in the limber.

Tuesday 20th
Forrest to lunch. Heard rumours that Bosch were going to attack. Forrest was now attached to Northants as 2nd in command.

Wednesday 21st
Went up to Hill Top Farm and waited for the Battn to come out of the line. They had gone in from Irish Farm two days before. Quiet night.

Thursday 22nd
Moved to Dambre Camp. CO, Cook and Gracie went on leave. Humphrey not well. Quiet night. Effie commanded Battn.

Friday 23rd
Humphrey stayed in bed. Quiet day.

Saturday 24th
Moved at 11 a.m. to Poperinghe. Good billets. Went to the Tivoli and saw the 32nd Div. Troupe 'The Pedlars'. Very good. The revue was written by Maurice Besley who was in the Footlights with me at Cambridge. I did not see him as he had left Poperinghe. Dinkie Fryer, Snodders Maxwell, Cross, Cunningham, Cartwright and Best arrived. The first two rejoining and the rest joining the Battn.

Sunday 25th
Brig.-Gen. Kemp came in. Tea with Doc at Skindles. Town Major (who was once in the Battn) came to dinner. Band played. Chug Chambers came back from Houtkerque.

Monday 26th
FGCM at Northants. Had lunch there. Went to the Empire to see 'The Duds' – very good. Effie, Humphrey and Rob dined sumptuously with the Town Major. (From all accounts it was almost Roman.)

France

Tuesday 27th
Moved at 8.25 a.m. to Herzeele. HQ officers billeted in a delightful convent. The Mother Superior was charming and did all she could for us. We all slept in a row in a long room with a lattice window opposite each bed. An unfortunate contretemps occurred while going to bed owing to a rag between Rob and Fletcher. Fletcher's sheets became drenched and he therefore had to hang them on

the bannisters outside and sleep in blankets. The Mother Superior was much hurt next morning as she thought we had considered her sheets not clean.

Wednesday 28th
Went to an ASC Cinema in a barn. Good.

Thursday 29th
Went to cinema. Very good.

Friday 30th
Effie and Humphrey dined at Cassel.

December

Saturday 1st
Went round to C Coy Lewis Gunners (about 2 miles away). Elsie and Dinkie to dinner. Effie and Cherry out to dinner.

Sunday 2nd
Went to Vol. Church in cinema. Effie, Humphrey and Fletcher rode to Cassel to lunch.

Monday 3rd
Went to 2nd Bde HQ to do Bde Major's job as Chichester Constable went to 35th Div. as GSO II. Went to cinema in evening. Not very good. Lt.-Col. Belamy (2nd Royal Sussex) was commanding the Bde.

Tuesday 4th
Tea with the Battn. Gordon Cummings (Staff Capt.) went to new area near Woesten to do the billeting.

Wednesday 5th
Stephenson (LNL and attached to Bde HQ) came back from leave. Went through mess a/cs with RQMS Crabtree.

Thursday 6th
Went to cinema and saw Billie Burke and Trudy Shattuck. Battn moved to Noyon Camp just NE of Crombeke.

Belgium

Friday 7th
Moved to Crombeke. Rode Kitty and fell off in front of the entire Battn of Northants.

Saturday 8th
Babe Buckland came back fróm leave (he was also attached to Bde HQ) so returned to the Battn. Effie, Elsie and Fletcher set off on leave in the dog-cart. Very dark narrow roads and they didn't know the way to Rail Head. CO Cook and Gracie returned. Went to Rousbrugge-Haringhe with Dinke.

Sunday 9th
The remains of the French Cavalry, from whom we had taken over the camp, moved off. Wet day.

Monday 10th
Took over map of the whole front to Bde HQ to put in the new line. Humphrey went on leave.

Tuesday 11th
Footer match v LNL. 1 all. Started writing a pantomime (in verse) at the CO's request.

Wednesday 12th
Moved to La Bergerie (Elephant) Camp in a little wood NE of Wogsten. This was a delightful little camp made of huts, dug-outs, elephant shelters etc., all very well camouflaged by the French. It was rather cold, but in summer must have been charming.

Thursday 13th
Ormrod and Harmon came back. Dined with A,B and D Mess. C had a mess of its own a little further off and more secluded.
[It was a source of annoyance that C Coy always got this when-ever we returned to the Camp.]

Friday 14th
Cherry came back. Ormrod and Hill went up to look round the line.

Saturday 15th
Dined in A, B, D Mess.

Sunday 16th
Went to Bde after lunch but met 'Steve' on the way. Tea with C Coy. Read to dinner.

Monday 17th
Went to Div. Concert Party in Woesten with Dinkie who came back to dinner. Ormrod left for the 11th Battn.

111

Tuesday 18th
Conference re taking over the line in the evening. Had a bath and shivered afterwards.

Wednesday 19th
Very cold. Moved up to Support Area on the Bixschoote–Langemarck road. Started at 2.30 p.m. Arrived about 6 p.m. and relieved the SWB. Didn't feel very well. Walked up with the Doc and another man.

Thursday 20th
Took over right sector of the Divisional line (in SW front) of Houlthoust Forest. The duck-board track was supported three feet above the surface of the mud and water and had a hand rail. It was quite impossible to go up the line except on this elevated track as apart from rainwater and shell holes there were numerous *bekes* or streams all very much swollen. Relieved the 2nd Welsh. Major-Gen. came round to us in the support area before we moved and there was much disturbance because the drippings from the taps of the water cart had run across the road and frozen.

Friday 21st
Major-Gen. came in. Quiet day. Very misty and cold. Feeling worse. Doc took my temperature and said it was 101.8°. Told me to go to the Dressing Station in the morning.

Saturday 22nd
Went to Dressing Station and was told I should have to go further down as I had PUO. James, my servant, was bringing my kit down from the Battn HQ with Hill (OCC Coy). Shell hit both – Hill badly in the leg and James slightly where he sits. We all three went down to Dressing Station at Eykhoek. I went on to No. 1 FA Rest Station at Wormhoudt (France), arrived about 8 p.m. and put to bed (proper one) in the ground-floor room of quite a good house with massive gold chandeliers and picture frames containing oil pictures of various ancestors.

Sunday 23rd
Stayed in bed. V. comfortable. Rfm. Forlong arrived as my new servant (No. 3).

Monday 24th
Stayed in bed.

Tuesday 25th
Snowed. Stayed in bed.

Wednesday 26th
Got up after breakfast. Went out but began to snow so came back after quarter of an hour.

Thursday 27th
Got up after breakfast. One hour's walk. Went to 63rd (RN) Divisional Follies. V. good.

Friday 28th
Got up to breakfast. Went for walk and felt strong enough to eat chocolates.

Saturday 29th
Went to Cassel with Colquhoun (Black Watch) to lunch at the Sauvage. V. cold. Went to the Follies in the evening. Bought a new rubber bath as my Béthune one had begun to leak.

Sunday 30th
Had a good deep hot bath in the bathroom.

Monday 31st
Rejoined Battn at Noyon Camp at Crombeke. Watched soccer on hard frozen ground, LNL v a Belgium team. (The Belges held the line on the left of our Division.) Not very well after dinner so went to bed. McCluse and Kirtland arrived.

References

[1] An incident similar to this forms a central event in William Boyd's novel *The New Confessions* (Penguin, 1987).
[2] Deputy Assistant Director of Ordnance Services.
[3] Observation Post.
[4] Ravenscroft is referring to the German tactical withdrawal to their prepared positions known as the Hindenburg Line. They destroyed everything in the country they abandoned, leaving many booby traps.
[5] i.e. Quarter-Master branch.
[6] Assistant Provost Marshall, i.e. Military Police.
[7] Officially known as the Second Battle of Arras, it lasted until 16th May 1917. The Canadian Corps distinguished itself on Vimy Ridge.
[8] Inland Water Transport.
[9] Railway Transport Officer.
[10] Ravenscroft is referring to General Plumer's attack on the Messines Ridge, when 19 mines containing 500 tons of HE were blown.
[11] Army Service Corps Motor Transport.

[12] The Third Battle of Ypres (Passchendaele) started on this day. One of its objectives was to capture the Belgian ports, which were believed to be essential to the Germans for their submarine campaign. This objective was soon abandoned.

[13] No relation to BL Montgomery, later Field Marshal, who was at this time a captain.

[14] Expeditionary Force Canteen.

[15] Col. Sir Neville Chamberlain, 1856–1944, ex Indian Army.

[16] The Third Battle of Ypres (Passchendaele) officially ended 6th November when the 2nd Canadian Division took the ruins of Passchendaele village at a cost of 2,238 casualties.

[17] Knee-length double-breasted coat, worn by officers.

III

January 1st 1918 to April 11th 1919

1918

January

Tuesday 1st
Celebrated Christmas Day. Much food and sports. 8th Royal Berks' Concert Party gave 2 performances in the evening. All officers after a large dinner invited to Sgts.' Mess Smoker. Much noise, smoke and drink. The CO insisted on singing an impromptu duet with me. I didn't know what he was going to do next – or for that matter what I was going to do next. Crabtree an admirable host.

Wednesday 2nd
Little warmer and rain. Got a piano in the Mess. Started L Gun class.

Thursday 3rd
A and B Coys' concert and then C and D. The hut wasn't large enough for the whole Battn at once. I went to the latter.

Friday 4th
Cherry came to dinner.

Saturday 5th
Moved to La Bergerie Camp. Humphrey came back.

Sunday 6th
Handed over to Humphrey after lunch. LG Class.

Monday 7th
Babe Buckland to dinner. LG Class.

Tuesday 8th
Dined at Bde HQ. A few shells round about.

Wednesday 9th
Cherry came back from Bde. Cartwright and Birks (NN) (attached to us) came back.

Thursday 10th
Fired A, B and D Coys. LG Class on the Range. Sang to the gramophone in A, B, D mess after dinner.

Friday 11th
Fired C Coy. LG Class on the range.

Saturday 12th
Battn moved up to take over front line as before. I went to Transport Lines in a wood just NW of Woesten. Messed in wooden hut. Slept with Cook in an Armstrong hut. Thaw and mud.

Sunday 13th
Cold and Bright. Went round billets. Palmer left for MG course in England (for good).

Monday 14th
More snow which lay.

Tuesday 15th
Rain in torrents. 3 officers and 25 men flooded out of their huts. Latrines completely cut off by a raging stream.
    [Up in the Front Line the duck-board track was washed away. Ration party couldn't get up; Effie waded to the waist in a swirling river loaded with soaked rations. I think some men in the Bde were drowned.]

Wednesday 16th
Cleared up the mess and opened up drains etc. Johnson (now Bde Gas Officer) gave a lecture on gas. Cartwright became Div. Baths Officer.

Thursday 17th
Sneddon went on leave. Battn came out into support area. Cherry came down from the Battn.

Friday 18th
Sent McCabe off to hospital. Heard that Hill had died of wounds
(He was hit on 22nd December 1917). [News of his getting the MC
came through later.]

Saturday 19th
Got up concert in Church Army Hut 5.30 p.m. Sang 'Hole in her
Stocking' and 'Maud's Bathing Costume'.

Sunday 20th
Went to Div. HQ at Woesten to arrange about getting witnesses
for Mess Sgt.'s FGCM from Dunkerque[1]. Battn came back to
La Bergerie.

Monday 21st
Battn moved back to Noyon Camp. I went with Interpreter in
car to Dunkerque to arrange to bring witnesses. Came back
through delightful old town of Bergues. Joined Battn on my
return at Noyon.

Tuesday 22nd
Went to Div. HQ to discuss trial with Schwartze (XIV Corps Court
Martial Officer) 10 a.m. Drove in the dog-cart. Danced in evening,
and upset stove.

Wednesday 23rd
Went on horrible old push bike to St Sixte (a convent) Corps HQ to
see Schwartze. Chain came off the bicycle half-way but fortunately
met a junior officer of the Battn who exchanged bikes!

Thursday 24th
Went to Poperinghe to see 'The Pedlars' (32nd Div.). Very
good indeed. Dinner at Skindles. Effie, Dinkie, Doc and Cherry
formed the party.

Friday 25th
Arranged billets for the witnesses. Heard that we were to move up
on Sunday.

Saturday 26th
Went to Dunkerque in an ambulance to bring back a female keeper
of a wine shop, a bank clerk and the SM of the EFC. When I had
got them safely back the woman at first refused to go down a dark

avenue to the farmhouse where I had arranged to billet her. After some argument she consented and finally was quite pleased with her apartment. The bank clerk was billeted in the same house.

Sunday 27th
Battn moved to Dekort Camp near the Support Bde HQ E of Woesten and N of Elverdinghe. I had lunch and tea with the LNL in the next camp to Noyon as the great FGCM took place on this day. There were 4 lawyers present, one of whom went to sleep at once. After the trial the Court Martial officer gave me a lift to our Transport Lines and I rode on from there to the Battn. The Interpreter was detailed to take the witnesses back next day. Found Dekort Camp quite nice, but not quite so nice as La Bergerie.

Monday 28th
Dinner with A Coy. McCabe came back. CO took over 2nd Bde temporarily. Lees (2nd in command) left in command of Battn.

Tuesday 29th
Tea with D Coy. Tested L Gunners in morning.

Wednesday 30th
Tested L Gunners, Brig.-Gen. Kemp came round. Went to Bde after lunch.

Thursday 31st
Dinner with Dinkie (D Coy). Bank had rifle practice in the afternoon.

February

Friday 1st
Went to The Pedlars near Elvedinghe, very good. Jock Lloyd (APM), Elsie and Read to dinner. CO came back from Bde. Slept with Dinkie, Chug went on leave.

Saturday 2nd
Went to Div. HQ 9.15 a.m. to discuss the bringing out of instruments for our String Band. Lees, Gracie, Hancock and I jumped lifts to Ypres. Explored the place and jumped lift home.

Sunday 3rd
Went to Church in Recreation Hut.

Monday 4th
Went to 'The Pedlars'. Took 200 seats for the Battn for the next night. Dinner with C Coy.
[Heard just about this time that I had been mentioned in despatches.]

Tuesday 5th
Golding came back. Humphrey and Read gave a joint dinner in the Recreation Hut. As usual it was smashed by the end of the evening. Whitewashed D Coy's mess with Dinkie.

Wednesday 6th
Heard that the Battn were going to side slip to the right and go in the line near Poelcappelle. Went down to the Transport Lines at Eykhoek in the dog-cart after lunch. Went with Rob to International Corner (Rail Head) after dinner in the trap to go on leave. Train left 12.26 a.m.

Thursday 7th
Arrived Calais 5.35 a.m. at Fontinettes Station and walked in the dark, wind and rain to the quay. Had breakfast at the Terminus Hotel on the quay. Went to see Winnie after. Embarked on SS *Dieppe* at 11.15 a.m. arrived Dover 1.50 p.m, left for Victoria 2.10 p.m.

Sixth Leave

Thursday 21st
Sick Leave.

March

Thursday 7th
Arrived Victoria 8.10 a.m. and got 1 violin, 1 cello and 1 bass out of the cloakroom. (I had collected them during the past few days.) Found the 8.30 a.m. cancelled so put them all back again.

Friday 8th
Arrived Victoria 8.15 a.m. Put the instruments in the van. The RTO once again tried to catch me for duty but I explained that I was not travelling light so he got someone else. Left 8.30 a.m. Arrived Dover about 10.15 a.m, lunch at the Grand Hotel. Left about 4.30 p.m. on SS *Dieppe* and arrived Calais about 6 p.m. Put the instruments in the Terminus Hotel. Met Snodders

and Cunningham. Took Winnie and Miss Ellis to dinner at the Continental. Slept at Terminus.

Saturday 9th
Lunch at Terminus. Saw *Count of Monte Cristo* on the film with Winnie and Miss Ellis. Tea with Winnie in her Mess (FANY)[2]. Took them to dinner at the Metropole. Bought music stands.

Sunday 10th
Lunch with Miss Ellis at Continental, (Winnie in bed with flu). Rode in open cab loaded with instruments to Fontinettes Station, left there about 3 p.m. Arrived Elverdinghe about 7.30 p.m. Went to Transport Lines and slept there. Left big instruments at the station. (Transport lines S of Elverdinghe.)

Monday 11th
Called at Div. HQ and Bde HQ. Rode up to the Battn at Kempton Park (a camp S of Pilkem on the Pilkem–Ypres road). Found Humphrey in command and heard that Paul Willmott had been killed while I was on leave. Took over Adjt. from Daniel Gurney.

Tuesday 12th
Looked at new Army Reserve Line and AA Lewis Gun at Kitchener's Wood near Boschcastle. New Brig.-Gen. (Kay, 60th Rifles) and Fergusson (new Staff Capt.) came up. Eddie Campbell and Michael came up in the dog-cart. Div. Band played in afternoon.

Wednesday 13th
SOS on our left at 2.30 a.m. Stood to. Very cold. Quiet about 3.30 a.m. Went back to bed. Fine day. Read came back. Cook went on leave. SOS again on left. Stood to for a short time.

Thursday 14th
Drill in the morning. Mason came back. Horrible noise all round at midnight.
   [Everybody had wind up just now as thought Bosch were going to attack, and SOSs went up on both sides at the slightest provocation.]

Friday 15th
Several visitors from 13th Battn. Went to Bde HQ in the morning. Looked round pill boxes in the Army Line in the afternoon. SOS on left about 9 p.m.

Saturday 16th
Took over front line (left sector of Bde front) at Poelcappelle from
1st SWB. Left Kempton Park at 7.15 p.m. Relief complete about
11 p.m. B Coy worried by TMs. Battn HQ at Norfolk Houses.

Sunday 17th
Fine day. B Coy at Requettes Farm, heavily strafed. Expected a
raid. A temporary officer of B Coy overdosed with rum. Hunter,
Cotton and Kinnear arrived.

Monday 18th
Brig.-Gen. Kay hit. [Afterwards died of wounds[3].] SOS on Requettes
Farm. Much noise. Winter (A Coy) was out with a patrol in both the
Bosch and our barrages, but got back afterwards without loss.

Tuesday 19th
Rain. Many shells and TMs during the night. GOC Bde and Div.
came in. Sussex came up to arrange relief.

Wednesday 20th
Enemy attempted to raid Requettes and Kettering at 2.30 a.m.
Elsie rushed up a reserve platoon to attack the Bosch in his front
posts but found his own platoons still there. Chug brought up
some SBs in the midst of the barrage and met Humphrey with
the remark 'Parlous times'. Caught 3 prisoners (one died), one
of whom was exactly like Hindenburg. Bde were much annoyed
because we sent in a report 'Hindenburg captured'. Harmon was
out on patrol in the middle of all this.

Relieved in the evening by Sussex, heavy shelling before we
left. Relief complete by 10.15 p.m. Walked back with Humphrey
to Hugan Hollows (Battn HQ), were shelled slightly. Before we
got there SOSs went up all round the salient. We turned round
and watched the finest display of fireworks (Bosch and Pain's)
ever seen. Every colour, rockets, golden rain etc. N, E and S of
us. Companies were scattered. Some living in Marine View and
others in Pheasant Trench.

[An American Officer with nigger blood in him, joined us for
a few days for instruction. On his arrival in the HQ pill box
he first produced cigars from his respirator for all of us and
then packet after packet of chocolate from the same place.
This caused amusement as there were very strict orders that
nothing whatever should be kept in the Respirator except the gas
mask.]

Thursday 21st
Great Bosch offensive down south[4], and *not* in front of us after all,
began. Sunny day. Battn bathed. All badly gassed in the evening
but no casualties. Humphrey who was at Bde HQ at the time would
ring me up to know if we were all right and I had to take my mask
off to answer him.

Friday 22nd
Sunny day. Relieved Northants in the right sector Battn HQ at
Hubner Farm [the large pill box mentioned on 13th November
1917]. Left at 8 p.m. Relief complete by 10.15 p.m.

Saturday 23rd
Quiet, warm and sunny. A and D Coys had Burns Houses as Coy
HQ. (Our old Battn HQ in November).

Sunday 24th
Lt.-Col. Kelly returned and took command of the 2nd Bde.
Humphrey took the American for a walk around the posts. At
one point they had to lie flat on the ground while MG bullets
whizzed over them about a foot above. 'Gee! This beats Hell',
murmured the Yank. At another they thought they had come upon
a Bosch post. Humphrey drew his revolver and moved on. 'Wait till
I get my Gat', said our guest. (We supposed he meant Gattling gun.)
[He left us the next day and was quite frank saying that he had had
enough of it already. We were quite sorry to lose him.]

Monday 25th
Chad (Adjt. of Sussex) and Upton (Sussex Sig. Officer) came up to
arrange relief. While strolling round some old Bosch gun pits I
found a lot of revolver amunition in curved clips holding 10 rounds.
The clips were similar to the ordinary rifle clips. There were still
a good many bodies lying about from the fighting of October and
November.

Tuesday 26th
Relieved by Sussex. Johnson (who was DAA & QMG at Div. HQ
when I was there) was now their CO. Went to Hugan Hollows
area again.

Wednesday 27th
Took summary of evidence for officer's court martial. Heard we
were to move sideways to California Trench tomorrow. Went
to look at it.

Thursday 28th
Relieved by 1st Gloucester (3rd Bde). Very slow relief; there was no excuse as it wasn't the front line. Took over California Trench from 1st SWB.

Friday 29th
11 ORs of A Coy sleeping in one shelter were killed by one shell. Several good NCOs being amongst them. Worked on the Army line (Battle Zone) as we still thought the Bosch might attack. Shelled at night.

Saturday 30th
Moved some companies to a safer place. Shelled during the morning. Doc Ward rejoined us after being a prisoner in Germany for 6 months[5]. He had been exchanged. Played ring quoits. Buried A Coy's dead in the evening. Had a proper service with 'Last Post'. Rain.

Sunday 31st
HQ and one Coy moved to good dug-outs with electric light on the Canal Bank by Brielan. Left the other companies forward. Lees rejoined the Battn. Winter got the MC.

April

Monday 1st
Warm, spring morning. C Coy came down from the forward area. Cook came back. Dined at Bde HQ.

Tuesday 2nd
Busy day. CO's conference at 6 p.m.

Wednesday 3rd
Other two Coys came back to Canal Bank. Prosecuted at GCM on officer. Effie came back. Soccer HQ v Sussex HQ. We won 6–1. Willan came in. Heard we were to move South on the 8th.

Thursday 4th
Eddie came back. Heard that we were to move either tonight or early next morning. Hectic day of orders and counter-orders. General excitement about where and when the Bosch were going to attack next.

France

Friday 5th

Moved at 8.40 a.m. to Boesinghe to entrain for Merville where we were to support the Portuguese. Billeting party went on by ambulance. When train got to Hazebrouck it went off on to the Béthune line. Terrific excitement on my part when the train stopped at Lillers. Got out and saw a good deal of damage done by bombs. We finally detrained at Choques. Marched to Lapugnoy where we arrived just after the billeting party. They had gone to Merville and then fresh orders had reached them. We all sat in the street until they had found us all billets which were good, had sheets on my bed. Quite forgot all about the Bosch's offensive in the excitement of being in the old area of 1915 and 1916.

Saturday 6th

Bicycled to Lillers through Allouagne. Saw my old friends and had my hair cut, but unfortunately the girl had moved to an inferior shop so my wants were attended to by a mere man. Tea at the Hotel du Commerce. Rode home in the rain. Mess dinner with champagne (dry).

Sunday 7th

Battn moved off by lorry to the old trenches just S of La Bassée Canal at Cambrin. (The Battn had been there before I joined them in 1915.) I moved off with Details (Effie in command) by road through Béthune and Beuvry to Le Preol (E of Béthune), about 2 miles behind the front line. Civilians were living there and also at Cambrin and had done so during the whole war. I really felt quite an old soldier now as I was the only officer (except Rob[6], the QM) in the Battn who had been continuously with the Division since they left the comfortable trench system, with sheets on beds within two miles of the line, in 1916. Explored in the evening. Rob, Effie and I shared a bedroom each having a good bed with the aforesaid sheets. Gas and ordinary shells at night. The area had just become lively (since March 21st) and some of the civilians were leaving.

Monday 8th

Went up to see the Battn at their HQ in Harley Street, Cambrin. Went through Annequin. Humphrey wasn't very well so it was arranged that I should relieve him on the next day.

Tuesday 9th

At 4.15 a.m. a terrific bombardment by the Bosch began[7]. Every gun went off at the same second. [A very clever piece of synchronisation]. We all leapt out of bed and found a thick mist and day trying to dawn. Shells were dropping all round the house but the mist was so thick that we couldn't see any of them. There were a lot of trees all round and the noise echoed through them in the most startling manner. We lighted a candle and started to dress. I was quite certain that the house would come down before we had finished. However, the house remained standing and it gradually got light, but the mist remained. We could get no news of any description, we had no telephone and any orders would have to come from Forrest who was commanding Bde Details at Le Quesnoy about a mile west.

During the morning a despatch rider on a motor-bike said he heard that the Bosch had broken through N of the Canal. This set us thinking. We didn't want to find ourselves attacked from the rear or left flank. We still didn't know whether the Battn was being attacked up at Cambrin. Our strength consisted of about 5 officers and 40 ORs apart from the QM's men and transport men. The QM stores were cut off from us as they were some way away and the barrage was too thick to penetrate. About 11 a.m. the mist cleared off (it may have been earlier) and still no news. It was then quieter. We had some food about 12 noon and then Read and I with two orderlies carrying rations set off for Bde HQ at Annequin Fosse. We thought it best to call in there on the way up to the Battn. (Read was to relieve one of the Coy officers.)

We walked along the tow-path of a branch canal running towards Annequin. Beuvry was being shelled with 11-inch (possibly more) and splinters were dropping into the water by our side from three-quarters of a mile away. We also had to pass one of our 6-inch batteries which, of course, was being shelled hard. One of the orderlies slipped and fell on the ration bag he was carrying. When he got up he was streaming with red – but he had only broken a bottle of red wine. We laughed for the first time that day. When we got on to the main Béthune – La Bassée road knots of civilians were standing outside their houses. They all appeared quite calm.

When we got to Bde HQ Kelly (GOC) wouldn't let us go up until he had rung up the CO. (Lees was commanding.) It was decided that Read should go up and that I should return to Details. (The Battn was perfectly safe in good dug-outs. They had been shelled of course, but not attacked.)

When I got back to our house at Le Preol I found one signaller only there. He said the remainder were in the swamp facing the canal in extended order. They had been told that the Bosch had definitely broken through N of the Canal.

[Chug had stalked up to the canal and looked over. He saw a party of Bosch approaching and thought 'Now for it', when he suddenly saw 2 Britishers marching at their head with fixed swords (bayonets). This relieved the situation somewhat and they all came back to their billets.]

Only Golding, Shaw and one OR were wounded during the day. Shaw afterwards died of wounds. We slept in our clothes and boots that night. Shelling continued in a lesser degree all through the night.

[Afterwards I heard that while the battle was at its hottest an old man and woman appeared on the tow-path riding bicycles westwards for dear life. Both sides stopped firing in amazement and I believe they got out of it safely.] Went round to see Forrest and hear what had really happened but he knew little more than we. Bde was far too much occupied to worry about Details. [The Bosch had taken Givenchy but were pushed out again later.]

Wednesday 10th
Heard at 8.30 a.m. that we were to move back to Burbure (near Lillers) at 9 a.m. and the transport was to move back to Annezin (near Béthune). Got off as soon as we could after loading the baggage, the Bosch speeding us with 5.9". Marched through Béthune, Choques and Allouagne and arrived tired but happy at 3 p.m. Delightful bed in room shared with Effie and good mess where the landlady made us the finest and biggest omelette ever eaten. Perfect peace after one of the most hectic days of my career.

Thursday 11th
Took Effie and Forrest to tea in Lillers at the Café with the three maidens and strawberry champagne [mentioned on January 15th 1916]. Bunny Head, Bass (Rhodesian), Garton and Harvie joined. (Bunny had hurt his knee in Paris last year and had retired to England.) Major Babcock (Attached LNL) was the senior major with Div. Details so he became OC Div. Details with ambitious ideas. (His HQ was to be known as Div. HQ.) Heard that we were to move to Marles-les-Mines.

Friday 12th
Moved at 10.20 a.m. to Marles-les-Mines through Allouagne and Lozinghem. Perfect day. Rather anxious about the War N of Béthune as continuous strafing went on. Continual streams of

traffic by road and railway going north. Watched many trains with men and guns (including Australians) passing through.

Walked through the Bois des Dames with Effie and Forrest. (This was the wood where we did wood fighting at the end of January 1916.) Watched the shells bursting in the plains south of Merville and Estaires. [The Bois was 60 metres above sea level – about 200 ft.]

Saturday 13th
Very cold and misty. Rly traffic greater than ever, all going North. Visited my old billet (July 4th 1916) with Effie. All delighted to see us. Anxiously asked if we thought the Bosch would shell their house as a new railway was being made from Marles to Lillers avoiding Chocques which passed next door. Gave us flowers from their garden.

Sunday 14th
Church Parade in school yard. Babcock much in evidence and collared me as his Adjt. Roney Kysles (Div. Padre) took the service. Heard we were to move to Gosney. Lt.-Col. Geoffrey St Aubyn arrived at the Battn in the line to take command.

Monday 15th
Moved at 2.30 p.m. to Gosney. Within the noisy area again. Comfortable but small billet. Transport joined us again there. Rob messed in a school yard amongst the stores. Lees came out of the line.

Tuesday 16th
Moved to Verquin. I went up the line to arrange Lewis Gun positions. Went round the Battn sector with Dinkie in morning and afternoon. Saw some of the tunnels that had been built during the last two years with electric light. The front line was not held continuously as before but a series of posts were held with tunnels leading to them. The old front line between them looked very desolate. They had fallen in and mines had been blown under it at various times. Met the new CO.

Wednesday 17th
Explored more tunnels. Went down in Padre's ambulance to Verquin after tea and found Details at the château built by a local brewer. Electric light and hot radiators. The owners had only left a week or so before. Played tennis on a hard court close to our

8″ which sometimes disturbed our strokes. Lees now commanding the 2nd Bde Details as senior major of Bde. Forrest to dinner.

Thursday 18th
Another great strafe in the early morning, but a little further off than on the 9th. The Bosch again attacked Givenchy. Many orders re standing to and moving. Definitely ordered to stand down about 8 p.m. Slept on first floor instead of second. Warner went up line.

Friday 19th
Quiet day – Bosch had failed – Effie went up line and Dinkie came down. 4 new L Guns arrived. Started new classes.

Saturday 20th
Northants took back the posts that the Bosch had taken on the previous day. Heard that we were to move at 4 p.m. to Raimbert. Eventually moved off in lorries about 7 p.m. Arrived 9 p.m.

Sunday 21st
Walked to Auchel in morning with Dinkie. Lovely day. Went to 55th Div. Concert Party Revue at 6 p.m. in Auchel with Dinkie and Lees. Very good girl as far as her voice went but bad clothes. Fuhr (ADMS) came to tea.

Monday 22nd
Heard that Lees had got command of the 18th Battn.

Tuesday 23rd
Lees left for 18th Battn. Effie and Cook came down, the latter to take over Town Major of Raimbert. Effie and I went to 55th Div. Revue in Fergusson's car.

Wednesday 24th
Moved early and suddenly to Mainil les Ruitz. The usual muddle over billeting. Nearly put under arrest by Babcock over a little matter of stabling accommodation.

Thursday 25th
Moved to Camp of Nissen huts in the Bois de Froissart between Bovigny and Aix Noulette. Very hot day. Marched through Barlin and Hersin.

Friday 26th
Misty day. Quiet. Noise at night. Good many shells passed over us to the mines and villages behind. SWB band played in the afternoon.

[The reason for all this moving was that when we were turned out of Le Preol we were in other Divisional areas, and as troops were being moved about a great deal and we had lost ground N of Béthune, no sooner had we settled in one village than the Div. whose area we were in wanted the village for its own troops. During the whole of this time the Battn was in the line. They had a fairly quiet time but they always had the feeling that the Bosch might turn his attention to them when he got fed up with N of the Canal. The men managed to get a bath during the period and a Regt canteen was opened in a dug-out.]

Saturday 27th
Moved at 2.30 p.m. to huts in the grounds of a château at Coupigny. Fletcher to lunch.

Sunday 28th
Gracie and Hancock came down from the line. Terrific noise all night.

Monday 29th
Cook came back from TM of Raimbert.

Tuesday 30th
Humphrey came in. Effie went up the line while CO dined at 1st Corps HQ (commanded by Holland who was our Div. Commander in the Winter of 1915/16. Went to 11th Div. Concert Party. Not very good. Asked if I should like to go to G Office[8] 1st Corps HQ to help during these strenuous times.

May

Wednesday 1st
CO and Humphrey came in. Did Mess a/cs.

Thursday 2nd
Moved to Noeux-les-Mines at 3.30 p.m. Halted outside for tea as the Camerons didn't move out till 7 p.m. CO, Humphrey, Elsie and HQ Coy came out of the line. [The rest of the Battn seemed to hold the line under Black Watch orders and with them, but evidently

came back to Noeux during the next 2 days. There are no further particulars in the original diary.]

Friday 3rd
Rode with Elsie through Bracquement, Petit Sains, Bully-Grenay to Maroc. Left horses with groom at our old Battn HQ for Maroc sector. Walked over the top to the Double Crassier and over that. Saw bones and bombs down the N side. These must have been the Sussex who went over with us on 30th June 1916. Imagined we were being sniped from N of Loos so got into Sap G and walked down the remains of Middle Alley. Rode home through Les Brebis. One of the most interesting afternoons ever spent. Saw Roy's grave at Maroc.
[The Canadians had advanced in this area in connection with the Battle of Arras in 1917.]
De Salis, Kiddle (Rhodesian), Davies, Elridge and Leith joined Battn.

Saturday 4th
Fired LGs. Went to Div. Concert Party. Our string band (less cellist who hadn't arrived yet) played very well. A new girl in the DCP (a Munster Fusilier), Cunningham and Chug came down from the line.

Sunday 5th
Sat on FGCM. Tried 8 cases. Forrest was President and came to dinner. Our string band played at Mess.

Monday 6th
Tried 9 more cases at FGCM.

Tuesday 7th
Called on Sussex LGO re new AA sights. Half HQ LG section disbanded. Conference for all officers. Mess Meeting. Band at Mess.

Wednesday 8th
Much wind up owing to a Bosch prisoner stating that Bosch were going to attack in the early hours, a feint bombardment was to start at 10 p.m. and the real one about 2 or 3 a.m. Dinner with A Coy. 10 p.m. arrived and went by with no strafe. Messy evening.

Thursday 9th
Great dinner at the HQ Mess. Cols. Robinson (Northants) and Johnson (Sussex) came. Military Band during dinner, bugle band

during coffee and cigars and string band after dinner. Rowdy evening. Received contents of full bottle of port as shampoo. A trifle sticky.

Friday 10th
Heard more about G office at 1st Corps HQ. Went to Div. CP. Our string band played.

Saturday 11th
Babe, Cherry (from Bde HQ) and Heyland (60th Rifles) commanding 1st Div. MG Battn to dinner. String band and dancing.

Sunday 12th
Busy day. Saw Corps Red Hats at Bde HQ. Battn took over right Bde, left Battn past Hohenzollern Redoubt. Details (of which I was one) moved to Huts in Bois d'Ohlain. A most delightful wood with birds singing but no furniture in the camp and no cookhouses. Went with Appsley (2nd in command of Sussex) to try and get furniture from Lindsay OC Div. MT Coy nearby.

Monday 13th
Rain. Went in car to Labuissières to 1st Corps HQ. Dined in E Mess in a hut by the side of the drive up to the château. The G office was in the château. Slept in a billet in the village nearby. Played bridge after dinner.

Tuesday 14th
Glorious day. Nothing very much to do. Studied the large-scale map of the Corps Front. I was here to help them during the strenuous time when the Bosch attacked and it would have been extremely interesting.
  [Unfortunately the Bosch didn't attack again.]

Wednesday 15th
Glorious day. Stayed in the office in the morning and after dinner. Walked in afternoon and went to 'The Archies' XIII Corps Concert Party. Very good girl of the Ethel Levey type but not pretty and had gold teeth.

Thursday 16th
Another glorious day. V. hot. Kinnear came over. Bosch plane downed near Beuvry.

Friday 17th
Similar day. Bosch knocked out 2 female tanks at Fosse 12.

Saturday 18th
Similar day.

Sunday 19th
Went in car with Board (Corps MG officer) to visit 46th and 11th MG Battns at Vauoricourt and Bracquement. (46th and 11th Divisions). Lovely day. Bosch set Béthune on fire with incendiary shells.

Monday 20th
Very hot indeed. Went out with Brig.-Gen. Hordern (BGGS 60th Rifles) and watched and criticised 1st Corps Cyclist Battn do a scheme at Hesdingeul. Béthune still burning. As fast as the REs (helped by the cyclists) put it out the Bosch set it alight again. The only way to put it out was to blow up the houses on the edge of the fire. It was very sad to think of that delightful town being absolutely destroyed after standing for 4 yrs of war.

Tuesday 21st
Very hot. One large shell dropped in a field behind the tennis court in the morning. Evidently a 'short' for Bruay. 2 Americans to dinner.

Wednesday 22nd
Went in car with Fanning to Château Le Pré, 2nd Bde HQ just N of Sailly Labourse and then on to tea with Details at Bois d'Ohlain. Then home through Ohlain, Rebreuve, Ranchicourt (1st Army HQ), Houdain, Haillecourt. Reconnoitred the road in case of sudden evacuation. Lovely scenery and very peaceful. Béthune on fire again.

Thursday 23rd
Bratten (Harrow and LNL) whose place at Corps HQ I'd taken, came back, so I prepared to return to my Battn. Walked through Bruay in afternoon, appalling dust and wind. More fires in Béthune. Dull morning but sun in afternoon.

   D Coy did a raid under Dinkie in the Hohenzollern sector. 4 prisoners and 1 MG captured. Many killed. Zero was 12.30 a.m. 23rd/24th. Corps very pleased. [Harvie wounded (died of wounds afterwards), Cotton and Garton also wounded.]

Friday 24th
Wet. Returned to Details in Bois d'Ohlain in Howard Jones' car
(GSO III 1st Div.). Dawson rejoined after a 6-month spell in
England. (He only did 3 months as a matter of fact).

Saturday 25th
CO and Dinkie arrived at Details which were now more comfortable. Fine day.

Sunday 26th
Fine and hot.

Monday 27th
Went to Houdain to see 'Les Rouges et Noir' 1st Army HQ pierrot
troupe. Quite the best and most artistic show I'd seen. Good theatre
(wooden) and wonderful production. A most perfect girl with red
bobbed hair and big brown eyes. Walked home in starlight through
delightful woods with Dinkie, Read and Daniel. Stood on the top of
the Ridge and watched the war up North.

Tuesday 28th
Battn came out of the line. Details joined them at Noeux-les-Mines.
The Mairie was the Battn Mess, a large hall with a platform at the
end. Very suitable for our string band.

Wednesday 29th
Started riding classes again in Transport Field under Fletcher.
Dined at 2nd Bde HQ.

Thursday 30th
Kelly (GOC 2nd Bde), Tandy (GSO I 1st Div.) and Splender Clay
(AA & QMG 1st Div.) dined. String band and bugles. Dancing
which turned into a horrible row. Humphrey started throwing eggs
about. When I (as financial Mess Pres.) expostulated he replied
with one full in my face, remarking that he had bought them
expressly for the purpose. As my features were becoming clogged
I retired for the night and endeavoured to set them free with water.
Needless to remark, I was not the only one who suffered. [In all
these rags our coats were always off, so they never suffered.]
    Went to Div. Concert Party in afternoon.

Friday 31st
Bosch shelled Fosse No. 3 near my AA LGs. Tea with 2nd TMB
Barnes (Sussex), late Bde Intelligence Officer, now commanding.
Merry evening with band and dancing.

June

Saturday 1st
Went to Div. Concert Party. Dancing and band after dinner.

Sunday 2nd
Lt.-Gen. Morland (60th Rifles), Brig.-Gen. Hordern and Brig.-Gen. Kelly attended Church Parade, March Past and lunch. String band at Church and lunch. I was at FGCM so didn't go to church. Gymkhana in afternoon, all the generals were there. We won 6 events. Jock Lloyd and Forrest to dinner. Terrific rag which annoyed the former and deprived the latter of his shirt.

Monday 3rd
Battn went to Bois d'Ohlain for a whole day field day. I fired LGs so didn't go. Several officers including myself had lorries to take us over to the 'Rouge et Noir' but found on arrival no performance. Dancing in evening.

Tuesday 4th
Went to Div. Concert Party in the Patronage 5.30 p.m. Danced 'Salome' to 'Valse Triste' in the evening.

Wednesday 5th
Battn took over Cambrin support area from 2nd Welsh. I went up as 'Works Officer', i.e. in charge of wiring and other unpleasant tasks. Half A Coy lent to Sussex and half A Coy lent to Northants. Wind up about a Bosch attack at dawn (6th June).

Thursday 6th
Breakfast at 2.30 a.m. so as to receive the Bosch on full stomachs. Tea with C Coy.

Friday 7th
More breakfasts at 2.30 a.m. for same reason. Wind down as nothing happened. Read got MC. Cambrin shelled in afternoon. Started wiring the Marsh between Annequin and the Canal in the evening. The Marsh was fairly dry now and the idea was to hold up the Bosch if he crossed the canal.

Saturday 8th
Big Bosch strafe in the evening.

Sunday 9th
Noisy day. B Coy relieved the two halves of A Coy.

Monday 10th
Quiet day.

Tuesday 11th
Quiet day.

Wednesday 12th
Misty morning. Fair amount of shelling. Dinkie and Read came to dinner. Woodruffe (2nd in command, Sussex) to lunch.

Thursday 13th
Quiet day. Relieved Sussex in Left Sector (canal to main road) (Cuinchy).

Friday 14th
Quiet day on the whole. British attack on our left some way north. Big noise. Dinkie got MC for raid.

Saturday 15th
Quiet day on the whole. Padre Clayton came to live with us. He slept with the Doc at Harley Street Dressing Station. Elsie came to see us from the Gunners where he was attached for a few days.

Sunday 16th
Went down from the line to take over temporarily Adjt. of 1st Div. Reception Camp at Bois d'Ohlain. Found Major Lochner (attached SWB) who was in command ill in bed in his tent with the three-day fever.

[This fever was at its height just about now. It affected all armies including the Bosch[9].]

Slept and messed with our Details in the Bois as the Reception Camp's quarters were not yet ready.

Monday 17th
Thunderstorm. Gracie went on leave. Div. Band played. Orderly Room Sgt. in bed with the fever, so I was in sole possession of the Reception Camp as far as Orderly Room was concerned. Splender Clay (AA & QMG) and Westley (DAAG) came round. Div. HQ after being shelled more than they liked in Barlin moved to Ruitz.

135

Tuesday 18th
Sports amongst all the Div. Details in the evening, but rain came on towards the end. Warner went on a course and Kinnear went to the MG school at Grantham.

Wednesday 19th
Sports postponed owing to the wet. Walked with Lochner to the Div. Concert Party at Maisnil les Ruitz.

Thursday 20th
Final day for sports. Rain stopped last two events. Effie came in. Snodders came down from the line.

Friday 21st
Battn relieved by 1st Bde. Details moved to Noeux-les-Mines. I moved to the new hut just built. Rain came through the roof. Tea with 1st SWB and dinner with LNL. Details.

Saturday 22nd
Lochner left for 74th Div. so Major Cunningham, senior officer with Details took command of the Reception Camp as well. (I did all the work.) Put up a lot of notice boards on the Ridge to keep people off the corn. Had breakfast (first meal) in the new Mess Hut. Very good food. Crutch (Welsh Fusilier, attached SWB) was the Gas Officer of the Reception Camp and was also made Mess President. He had an excellent cook (a Rfm. belonging to the 2nd Battn). Altered the roof of my hut and got covered in tar. (Tarred felt was used.)

Sunday 23rd
Div. Band played. Had a door fixed to my hut. Decorated the Mess and camouflaged the outside. Got the Mess gramophone back from SWB.

Monday 24th
Rain. Roof still leaked so put more felt and odd bits of corrugated iron on. Green (acting DAQMG) came to tea so managed to get a little more material out of him. Window (oiled linen) fixed to the hut.

Tuesday 25th
Splender Clay and Westley came in morning and S Clay and Hughes (DAQMG) came in afternoon.

Wednesday 25th
Walked through Verdrel in morning. Arranged with Canadian REs to get a better water supply. Kittermaster, who had just returned to the Div. as senior padre after having gone back to Harrow, came in to see me. Walked with Crutch to the top of the Ridge in the evening. Rather misty.

Thursday 26th
Major-Gen. inspected drafts of Black Watch and Camerons. Warmer day.

Friday 27th
Started digging a flower garden round the huts. Crutch an efficient gardener. Chug came to tea and told me practically the whole Battn had 3-day fever.

Saturday 29th
Quiet day.

Sunday 30th
Quiet day.

July

Monday 1st
The whole 2nd Bde was inspected by the Duke of Connaught near the Bois des Dames.

Tuesday 2nd
2nd Bde relieved the 3rd Bde in Hohenzollern sector. As Chug was the only 60th officer with Details he messed with us. Major-Gen. came round in morning and stopped the 3rd Bde Details from moving until the evening. 'Why move in the heat of the day?' said he. Div. Band played in the evening.

Wednesday 3rd
Hordern arrived to join the Battn. Cook and Winter came down from the line to go on leave. Cunningham (Black Watch) went up the line so Major Methuen (Camerons) became OC Camp.

Thursday 4th
Started draining our premises. Major Brudenell-Bruce (attached G Staff 1st Div.) took possession of my orderly room in the morning

without my knowing anything about it till I went in there, and told the various LG officers and Coy Commanders how to train their Lewis Gunners. He finished up a revolutionary syllabus by saying 'Of course I know nothing about Lewis Guns'. (I think really he was only the mouthpiece of the G staff.)

Friday 5th
Westley came round in the morning. Cartwright, Gracie (from leave) and Rob to lunch. Battn details now started their own mess. After tea a bare-headed officer from the Chinese Labour Corps nearby rushed into the orderly room and asked for 50 men at once as the Chinese were threatening to riot. 1 officer and 50 stalwart Camerons, complete with bagpipes, marched off. The affair, however, was settled before they reached the Chinks, so they returned home disappointed.

[The Labour Officer told me afterwards that the Chinks often had riots when they thought one of them was ill-treated by the British NCOs. They didn't mind bullets; in fact when they saw troops levelling their rifles, they would bear their breasts and, holding back their heads, rush towards the muzzles. They didn't like cold steel, however.]

Saturday 6th
Heard that the proper Adjt. of the Reception Camp was not coming back and that a BI officer from the Base was coming to relieve me.

Sunday 7th
Humphrey came to Details. Had dinner with him.

Monday 8th
Major-Gen. unavoidably failed to turn up for draft inspection. A composite company of all the oldest war soldiers of the Black Watch arrived. They were to go to Paris for some ceremonial purpose. Doc Aitcheson relieved Doc Fletcher at the Reception Camp.

Tuesday 9th
After many attempts got the water supply question settled. (Lack of rain had been the excuse.) Major-Gen. inspected Drafts and Black Watch composite Coy. No strafing.

Wednesday 10th
Lunch with Battn Details.

Thursday 11th
Relief day for the Brigades. Capt. Bruce (the BI officer) arrived to take over Adjt. Lt.-Col. Davenport arrived at tea-time to take command of the Reception Camp permanently. He had been in command of a Base Camp at Dieppe or Cherbourg.

Friday 12th
Showed Davenport and Bruce the various training grounds and explained the details of the view of the line from Lens to Kemmel from the Ridge. Kittermaster to tea and Humphrey to dinner.

Saturday 13th
Went with Chug, Barfoot (Sussex) and 'Sniper Bill' (Methuen Abe Bailey's SA sharpshooter attached for rations to Northants) to 'Rouge et Noir' at Houdain. Dined at Hotel du Centre. Met Roskill (Cambridge) at the Theatre. Watched the searchlights from the ridge on the way home.
   [Chug and I had become very fond of this part of the country and we often discussed settling down in the Château d'Ohlain and growing corn for a livelihood, with visits to Béthune for liveliness, after the War; with or without wives.]

Sunday 14th
Rode on push bike to dentist at 1/3rd West Lancs. FA[10] between Ruitz and Houchin. (Had wind up about a tooth but all was well.) Kittermaster to lunch. Much rain in afternoon.

Monday 15th
Went up the line with Cook. Tea with Rob in the cemetery at Noeux-les-Mines. Met JS Wilson (who was hit on 19th August 1916 at High Wood). He had come over from GHQ by car. Dined at Battn HQ, NE of Vermelles. Took over C Coy in support at Central Keep. CO went sick and Humphrey in command.

Tuesday 16th
Thunderstorm during the night (15th/16th). Quiet day. Very hot.

Wednesday 17th
Relieved B Coy in Right Sector of front line. Read (proper OC C Coy) came up and took command. My platoon in Bart's tunnel and Spool Keep. Very hot.

Thursday 18th
Quiet and hot day. Strafe at evening stand to and shelling all through the night. 11th Div. (on our right, our old area in February–June 1916) let off gas projectors.

Friday 19th
Inter platoon relief. Went back to reserve line.

Saturday 20th
Quiet day. Sussex did a raid on our left at midnight 20th/21st. Barnes (Sussex) OCTMB blown to atoms. Not a trace of him. A shell must have hit him and a pile of Stokes bombs by which he was standing.

Sunday 21st
Kings Liverpool (an ex-Labour Battn) 59th Div. came up for instruction in the morning. Relieved by Black Watch at 5.30 p.m, a daylight relief which was an untold blessing. (One of the great advantages of tunnels and good trenches.) Walked back to Noeux-les-Mines via Vermelles, Noyelles and outskirts of Mazingarbe (the village where I first joined the Battn in November 1915). Looked for Godfrey Hine's grave in Vermelles but couldn't find it. Mess at the Mairie again.

Monday 22nd
Went to cinema. Peter Davies to dinner from somewhere around Vimy. Told that the CO wanted me to be 2nd in command of C Coy. What a life!

Tuesday 23rd
Rained hard. Walked practically all the way to Houdain to get tickets for 'Rouge et Noir'. All seats sold for the remainder of our rest. Tea at the Hotel du Centre. Walked practically all the way back. However, very soothing to the nerves.

Wednesday 24th
Got up at 5 a.m. Marched to 'P.12.d' (my beloved Bois d'Ohlain) for a field day. Lovely day. Lunch in the wood. Forrest, Robinson (OC Northants), Woodruffe, Appsley (Sussex), Crutch, (Gas Officer Reception Camp), Cherry, Johnson and Hines (2nd Bde) all to dinner. Military Band at dinner and good sober dancing to string band afterwards. No horseplay!

Thursday 25th
Humphrey made Acting Major. Went to Div. concert party with Johnson who came to tea. They did 'A Sister to Assist Her'. Div. Band played at dinner. Went for a country walk with Chug afterwards and discussed whether we lived or merely existed.

[I hated going back to Company work after being on HQ for so long. I missed the information and knowledge of what was going on, and I didn't like not being my own master under the CO direct.]

Friday 26th
Innoculated. Wet day. Went with Cherry and Gracie to the 'Wunny Wuns' Revue and '5 (K)nights'. 11th Div. at Bracquement. Got wet coming home.

Saturday 27th
Rain. The CO came to tea from the FA Mess Meeting to discuss apportionment of drinks. [This happened at odd intervals, but nothing very much was ever done. I had ceased being Financial Mess President and Rob (QM) had taken on the whole job (both mine and Effie's).] Hodgkinson the cellist arrived at last. When he was sent out from England he was posted to another Battn. He got a LG stripe and became a Lewis Gunner. When our CO wrote to his CO asking for him, the reply was that he was too valuable to be spared and LGs came before cellos. We offered 2 L Gunners in exchange but no good. Even the Corps Commander wrote to his Corps Commander but no good. At last Hodgkinson went sick and went down the line. Div. then kidnapped him in an ambulance. Walked to Verquin to see the 'Whiz Bangs' concert party. Very good.

Sunday 28th
Horse and limber show. Rode with Chug to tea with Crutch at the Reception Camp. String and military band at dinner. Meares (new Bde Major), Cherry and Boutiel to dinner. Dancing, but rather flat.

Monday 29th
Chug, who had taken on my pet job of LGO ran a stripping etc. competition. I judged. Rain.

Tuesday 30th
Got up at 5.30 a.m. and went to Hersin Range. McCabe who was doing Adjt. to Humphrey went sick. I did (1) Adjt.'s work (orders for taking over the line tomorrow), (2) received my own orders as OC Coy, (3) got up and rehearsed a concert in the Patronage

141

(where I gave my first concert in December 1915) and (4) went to Bracquement to try and get Harry Welchman to sing at the concert. He was giving his show somewhere else and promised to come over afterwards if he got back in time, but he didn't. Finally, the concert itself at 8 p.m. Pretty strenuous day. Battn played 1st Corps at cricket. Humphrey broke his arm in a jumping competition.

Wednesday 31st
Took over Cambrin Support Area from SWB. Morning relief. I took in C Coy with Snodders, my senior and a Regular, under me. Most awkward. Billet by the Church. Battn commanded by Lt.-Col. Badham who was really attached to us for instruction as he had been out East.

August

Thursday 1st
Quiet. Walked to Vauxhall and Westminster Bridges over the La Bassée Canal. Stung by nettles. Very hot.

Friday 2nd
Rain. Short strafe right on us about 6.30 p.m.

Saturday 3rd
Rain, quiet day.

Sunday 4th
Relieved A Coy Sussex in left sector. Noisy night.

Monday 5th
Quiet day. Explored the lock and the railway embankment. Put a Platoon Sgt. and Cpl. under open arrest for being in a dug-out while on duty.

Tuesday 6th
Summary of evidence taken on my two prisoners. Kelly came round about 5.30 p.m.

Wednesday 7th
Quiet. Savin came back, and to C Coy. CO came back and took over command. Camerons did a raid on the right. Some retaliation.

Thursday 8th
Relieved by A Coy Sussex. Savin took 2 of my platoons to live at Pont Fixe – a horrible place on the canal – once a bridge. Always

being strafed. Remainder of Coy went to N Annequin (Cambrin Support Area). A few shells, bad cellars.

Friday 9th
Went round Islip Post with the two colonels.

Saturday 10th
Had a bath in the baths at N Annequin. An unpleasant proceeding as the Bosch shelled these baths suddenly and often, there were no cellars, and I objected to being shelled when I had nothing on, more, even, than when fully dressed. However, I completed my toilet this time undisturbed. Dined with A Coy. (Elsie and Bunny etc.) Discussed the belief or otherwise in the Bible or Hell.

Sunday 11th
Reconnoitred Support Line. S Annequin and Noeux-les-Mines shelled hard. It was most unusual for Noeux to be shelled. Not one shell had ever dropped in the village while I had been there either in 1915 or 1918.
[The Div. Band billet was hit and several bandsmen wounded and gassed and the LNL had to clear out a few nights later in the middle of the night and encamp in the fields behind.]
Dined with 2nd Bde HQ at Annequin Fosse and inspected new method of loading LG limbers.

Monday 12th
Went to Noeux for FGCM. Luckily it was not shelled while I was there. Very hot day. Lunch with Forrest who was now OC LNL and a Lt.-Col.
[The LNC were now in the 1st Bde. This alteration had been made a few months ago when the Infantry Bde was reduced to 3 Battalions.] Battn relieved Northants in Front Line. My Coy took over Carey's (Northants) in Support Line.

Tuesday 13th
Quiet day. Very hot. Beautiful trenches. Even cigarette ends were not allowed to be thrown on the trench boards, but had to be put in sand-bags hung for the purpose in every traverse.

Thursday 15th
Bomb dropped very close in Harley Street. Gurney and Hancock went over to the Bosch line to see whether it was occupied. Hancock was killed and his body could not be recovered. Gurney was hit in the left eye.

Friday 16th
Lister joined the Battn and Coy. De Salis came up to the Coy from Details. Went up to arrange relief.

Saturday 17th
Took over left front Coy from B Coy.

Sunday 18th
Read came up and took over the Coy. I went down by an ambulance train from Cambrin to Labourse to go on a Musketry Course at the 1st Army School. As my servant, Forlong, was on leave I took on Wilkins who had been Hancock's servant. Dinner with Rob. Rode over to Details at Bois d'Ohlain in the starlight. Very glad to get out of Noeux as the Bosch were shelling it every day and even Rob's house in the cemetery had had chips taken out of it. Saw Cazelet (Cambridge) who had come out with the reconstructed 16th Div. He was Bde Major and was going to take over our area. Bomb dropped 200yds away. A piece of impertinence, bombing our peaceful wood, but I think it was an accident.

Monday 19th
Lunched with Crutch. Listened to our string band in the afternoon. Went to 'Les Rouges et Noir' at Houdain in the evening.

Tuesday 20th
Walked to Barlin. Lorry left there 8.30 a.m. (an hour late) for Calonne Recouart. Train from there to Anvin. Lunch there with some 3rd Bde officers going on the same course. Metre gauge from there to Fruges. Changed there and on to Matringham. Arrived at 6.45 p.m. Charming Nissen hut camp with spring mattress beds (without sheets), shower baths, flowers, artistic mess. 5 of us in a hut for sleeping.

Wednesday 21st
V. hot. Opening address by the commandant. Very quiet and peaceful but some of the officers were pretty awful. Bad cooking.

Thursday 22nd
So hot that we paraded in the evening instead of afternoon.

Friday 23rd
Cooler day. A misguided PT instructor gave us a massed boxing lesson. My partner (or opponent, I should say) was a very young

and sprightly Scottish Rifleman who had evidently had some previous lessons.

Saturday 24th
Half holiday. Little rain. Walked to Fruges after lunch with Mackintosh (Camerons). Tea and dinner at Hotel Moderne. Bad beer at the Cheval Noir. Got a lift back in RAF tender.

Sunday 25th
Spent quiet peaceful day in the sun in a deck chair. Read 'Guy and Pauline' in the proper atmosphere. Not very well inside owing to some minced bully beef. (Several of us had ptomaine poisoning.)

Monday 26th
'Very Lights' (1 Corps pierrot troupe) gave a show. Harry Welchman was in it. Quite a good girl was also in it (imitation, of course).

Tuesday 27th
Went to 'Very Lights' again. Getting very fed up with the Course. Treated like a child by a Sgt. who had never been near the line. Several loathsome so-called officers in my section.
[When McCabe, who was doing Adjt. had told me that I was to go on this course I implored him to get the CO to send someone else, but he said I hadn't been on a course for over 2 years and there was no-one else.]

Wednesday 28th
Lecture by Lt.-Col. Campbell, the PT expert. Lorry to Fruges to see 'Les Rouges et Noir' but they didn't do such a good show as they did in their own theatre. Dinner at Hotel Moderne. Back by same lorry.

Thursday 29th
Fired grouping practice.

Friday 30th
Had first exams. Re-organisation of the Coys as two instructors left for a 'rest' in England.

Saturday 31st
Played for 'England' against Scotland, Wales and Ireland at Rugger. 3 all. Lena Ashwell's concert party at 8 p.m. Free. Quite a good show of its kind. 3 girls (real) and 1 man.

September

Sunday 1st
Quiet day. Walked with Green (3rd Bde) to tea (fresh boiled eggs) at Vincly, 1 kilometre away.

Monday 2nd
Portuguese officers visited the camp and we had to perform on the miniature range for them.

Tuesday 3rd
Ordinary procedure.

Wednesday 4th
Fired on 200yds range.

Thursday 5th
Very hot.

Friday 6th
Very hot. More exams.

Saturday 7th
Demonstrations on the range for a party of Battn Commanders who seemed as bored as I was.

Sunday 8th
Wet. Walked with Green to Senlis and back.

Monday 9th
Rain. More exams.

Tuesday 10th
Rain. Went by train to Fruges with Harris (LNL). Tea and dinner at Cheval Noir. Walked back.

Wednesday 11th
Rain in morning. Rugger, played for England v Scotland and Wales (another injustice to Ireland). Lost 11–0.

Thursday 12th
Rain. Got up at 5 a.m. Left Matringham 7 a.m. arrived Anvin about 10 a.m. RTO hadn't the slightest idea where the 1st Div. was now as they had left the Béthune area; so he told us we had all

146

(officers and other ranks) better go to Etaples where we could find out! No expense spared. Lunched at Café opposite station. Train about 5 p.m. Dinner and slept at officers' club. Sheets. There were curtained cubicles in a long hut. A pretty rowdy lot of officers there too. Terrific argument between two drunk ones with by-play by several others less so. The chorus seemed to be 'I'm as good a man as you and I'll prove it now'. Occasionally a sleepy curse would be heard from the other end of the hut telling them to be quiet. Much as I loathed the proximity of the Bosch I almost longed to be back with the Battn.

Friday 13th
Fine. Went by train to Paris Plage with Walker (3rd Bde) and Mackintosh. Came back through Le Touquet. Dined at the officers' club.

Saturday 14th
Tried to get a pass for Boulogne with Walker. Various orderly rooms said they had no objection but the other orderly room would give us the pass. Went off by lorry at last without one. Dinner at Mony. Returned by tram to Pont les Briques and caught a passenger train to Etaples to avoid RTOs. Had a sit-down bath (white). Rain.

Sunday 15th
At last we found out where the 1st Div. was. Left at 11 a.m. and arrived Villers Brettoneux (now in ruins) at 4.30 p.m. Passed through Abbeville and Amiens. Marched to Corbie where the Reception Camp and Battn Details were. Found McCabe in charge of our Details in miserable circumstances. His first words were 'Have you brought your rations?' They just had the necessaries of life but not a drop of the liquid necessaries, and this after a 3-mile hot and dusty walk. Went to see the Reception Camp but they were no better off.

[This was the beginning of weeks of living in utter desolation – not a whole house, not a civilian, not a complete tree for miles in any direction.]

Monday 16th
Left Details about 9.15 a.m. and walked with Forlong (my servant) most of the way to Villers Bretoneux. Found a broken wheelbarrow amongst the ruins and took turns at wheeling my valise from the station to the main road. It was a dreadfully hot day. Waited at the

crossroads for a lorry. Finally got one to Villers-Carbonnel. Waited an hour there and got another to Mons en Chaussée. Dumped the kit there and left Forlong to look after it, and proceeded to find the Battn. Walked through Estrées en Chaussée and along the road towards Tertry. Eventually found Crabtree with our 2nd line Transport. He directed me on to Caulaincourt Wood. Arrived about 7 p.m. to find the Battn were moving up the line for an attack in the evening. Had dinner with C Coy in the wood. Shelled with gas shells just as the Battn were moving off. I remained with Battle Reserve and only moved about quarter of a mile forward. Slept with Chug in a small shelter.

[During my absence the Battn had helped the Canadians at Arras and had suffered heavy gas casualties.]

Tuesday 17th
Quiet day. Much bombing round about at night. Had a look round in the morning. Went E of Vermand with Humphrey and Chug to look at the Bosch lines in the distance.

Wednesday 18th
Battn attacked and took Berthaucourt. Zero 5.20 a.m. [Elsie badly hit, Eldridge and Best killed and Winter and Lister wounded.] The CO hit slightly in foot. Elmhurst and Simmonds joined. Padre came in with rumour that Elsie had been killed which upset all of us, especially Chug.

Thursday 19th
Chug went up the line without orders. Cunningham died of wounds.

Friday 20th
Marlowe missing. Chug hit in the face. CO returned to duty from CCS. Battn relieved by a Bde of the 46th Div. I went to Montecourt to do the billeting but on the way back met the Bde Major who said we would not be going back after all. Wake joined Battn. Total casualties for the tour: 8 officers and 153 other ranks.

Saturday 21st
Quiet day. Gen. Kelly came to tea. White joined the Battn. (Not the same White as at Le Clipon.) Bill Dawson came up from Details late at night.

Sunday 22nd
Padre Clayton preached his last sermon before going to the Base.
Rain and conference in evening.

Monday 23rd
Moved up the line in charge of No. 9 Platoon C Coy (each Coy
had only 2 platoons now) under Cook (OC Coy) at 10.55 p.m.
through Vermand, Villecholles, Maissemy to take up positions for
an attack next morning. Gas shelled rather badly at the spot where
we off-loaded the limbers. Arranged my platoon with the help of
white tapes in shell-holes in front of line held by Duncan's Coy
Black Watch. Long hours of waiting. My morale very low indeed.
Quite sure my turn had come to stop some of the Bosch's metal.
  [The fact of once again being a platoon commander may have
accounted for this.]
  We were to go over behind the Sussex and then make a right
turn and get on their right.

Tuesday 24th
Issued rum at 4.30 a.m.[11] Zero 5 a.m. Got into the Bosch trenches
without much difficulty. Our barrage was good but far too much
smoke: it not only prevented the Bosch from seeing us but it
prevented our seeing our direction or anything else. Took a lot
of prisoners whose morale was very low. Went down the wrong
trench but eventually found the right one. Fairly quiet about 8
a.m. The people on our right could not get on at all and we were
very nearly left in the air. Fired several LG magazines at crawling
Bosch at about 800-yards range to our right rear, but don't think I
got any of them. There was too much cover. Told to take over B Coy
at 11.30 a.m. Got in touch with 3rd Bde on right about 12 noon.
  Some Camerons came up in the afternoon to take over my
position as we had to go forward. They were shelled hard all the
way and an awful block in the trenches. 5.9"s in profusion. After
moving from place to place finally took up a right position (just in
front of the only dug-out which Battn HQ took). The Bosch shelled
pretty hard.
  Had a horrible job at night searching shell-holes etc. on the left
for suspected Bosch and finding touch with the Northants. Wake
killed, Dawson, Davies and Cotton wounded.

Wednesday 25th
Shelled most of the day. A and C Coys were on a ridge about
half a mile in front. Bosch tried to counter-attack them. I stood
looking over the parapet all day waiting to see either the Bosch

or an SOS in which case I was to rush up to the rescue. Three good SBs buried alive. Hit about 5 p.m. on the chin with shell splinter. Lot of blood but not deep. Went to dressing station and left Drakin in command. I'm not subject to hysterics but the sudden end of the responsibility and the all-day watching made me talk a lot of drivel at the Battn HQ. Walked down via Essling Alley and Villemay Trench with Forlong to Maissemy Dressing Station. Ambulance with wounded Bosch to a Main Dressing Station somewhere. Finally an ambulance lorry to 47 CCS at Brie. A most unpleasant day but not as bad as the Somme.

Thursday 26th
Arrived 47th CCS at 12.30 a.m. Stayed in bed. CO came into the opposite bed being hit in the head. McCabe, Snodders, HH Robinson and Burrowes came in to see me from their Details Camp close by.

Friday 27th
Got up for tea. Walked to Div. Reception Camp.

Saturday 28th
Got up for tea. Cold and rain. The CCS was of canvas but very comfortable.

Sunday 29th
Got up after lunch. Cold.

Monday 30th
Left the CCS and joined Details. [I had to argue hard so as not to be sent down the line; but really hadn't the face to go down with my scratch.[12]]
   Slept with Crutch (Div. Reception Camp Gas Officer) in a comfortable elephant shelter. Dinner at Reception Camp. CO arrived back from the Base Hospital as he couldn't stand it and went up to join the Battn.

October

Tuesday 1st
Effie arrived back. Rain. Started building a Mess.

Wednesday 2nd
Details Sports in afternoon. Cold and a little rain. Continued building the Mess.

Thursday 3rd
Went up with Effie (jumping lorries) to the Battn at Vermand. Very hot and sunny. Told to train more Lewis Gunners. Slept in a tent with Scatter (a new officer) in the odour of at least one dead horse (the hoofs visible).

Friday 4th
Marched off at 7 a.m. in Fighting Order to bivouac round about Sampson Trench (where I was hit). 6″ now up there firing all out and swarms of horses, balloons, etc. On arrival we were told to go back again as the Division had been Squeezed out (11.30 a.m.). Halted for dinners at Vermand cemetery at 2 p.m. Arrived Caulaincourt village (remains) on the top of the hill about 4.30 p.m. Enjoyed the day on the whole. Slept with Fletcher and Gracie in draughty hut. Brig.-Gen. Kay (60th Rifles) and his Bde Major 3rd Bde killed.

Saturday 5th
Cherry rejoined Battn from Bde HQ. Started LG classes in the Chapel of the Marquis de Caulaincourt.

Sunday 6th
Church Parade 10 a.m. Kelly and Strickland made speeches afterwards. CO left to command the 3rd Bde. Effie came up from Brie to command Battn. Very windy. Kay's funeral.

Monday 7th
Heard Battn was to move up the next day. Left Battn at 4.30 p.m. for leave. Got lift in Aitcheson's ambulance to Brie. Slept and dined with Details. [This last week I hated more than any other. Had a feeling that I was no longer any use in the Battn.] Had a heart-to-heart talk with Mac at Details on things in general, and ourselves and the Battn in particular.

Tuesday 8th
Got to Brie Station 7.30 a.m. Train arrived 9 a.m. Arrived Boulogne 9 p.m. Very slow. Had an interesting talk with an Australian MG Colonel on the Americans at the Canal du Nord. Slept and dined at Hotel de Paris.

Wednesday 9th
Left Boulogne about 10.30 a.m. Folkestone 1.15 p.m. Left at 1.50 p.m. Arrived Victoria 4 p.m.

Seventh Leave

Wednesday 23rd
Left Victoria for Folkestone at 8.10 a.m. By some mischance the train arrived at Dover at 11 a.m. At first the RTO wanted us to go back to Folkestone but eventually we left Dover on the *Duchess of Argyll* at 6.30 p.m. having lunched with MacNaught (Adjt. of Northants) at the Grand. Dined and slept at the Hotel de Paris, Boulogne with MacNaught.

Thursday 24th
Left Boulogne with only coffee inside at 7.47 a.m. Forrest travelled in our carriage. Arrived Vermand via Amiens and Roisel at 9 p.m. Lost my wristwatch. Slept at the Reception Camp, Vermand.

Friday 25th
Left Vermand at 11 a.m. and lorry-jumped through Belleglise, Fresnoy le Grand, Bohain, Busigny, Vaux Andigny to Wassigny. Arrived about 4.30 p.m. Awful noise of our 6-inch Navals firing all out. Tea and dinner at Battn HQ. Atmosphere totally different from when I left the Battn a fortnight ago. Humphrey was commanding during the absence of Effie. Judd was attached to us for instruction in our sort of warfare after having served in German Africa. Took over A Coy (my old Coy) as proper Company Commander. Went to see Sladen who had rejoined during my leave. A few Bosch shells at night.

Saturday 26th
Went over the battlefield of Vaux Andigny which the Battn took part in on the 17th October. Very glad I missed it as we seemed to have had a pretty hot time, and lost a good many. Quite a hot day. Heard we were to go up the line tomorrow.

Sunday 27th
Reconnoitred the line on the Canal de la Sambre between Rejet de Beaulieu and Cambresis. Quiet and sunny. This sector was most extraordinary. We had isolated posts practically up to the Canal which had a reservoir on each side. There were tiny fields, most of them not greater than 100 yards x 50 yards with thick hedges and a lot of trees. There was nothing to suggest a front line. The trees were full of autumnal foliage and no shell-holes were visible. Nobody quite knew whether any Bosch were on our side of the Canal or not. Took up the Company in the evening and relieved the LNL in the centre Coy front. Caught

in a bad strafe between Battn HQ and Coy HQ going in across a field. No cover. Lost 3 good stretcher-bearers killed, and 2 other men wounded.

Monday 28th
Quiet and sunny. Walked down the Canal Bank. No sign of the Bosch and no sniping, but at the lock on the left Coy's front there was a good deal of it.

Tuesday 29th
Pallett went out with three men exactly as I had done the day before and had a MG turned on them at close range. They were all hit and had a most unpleasant time getting in as every time they moved the Bosch fired at them. Coy HQ shelled hard during the day. Various new posts established.

Wednesday 30th
Very heavy shelling of Coy HQ and several direct hits but cellars stood intact. (It was an old Bosch Dressing Station). Relieved by 2nd Welsh. Relief complete about 6.30 p.m. Marched back to Vaux Andigny, arrived about 10 p.m. Comfortable bed but squashy. 2 of us slept and ate in the same small room. Effie arrived back and assumed command. Now a Lt.-Col.

Thursday 31st
Went to Div. Concert Party and string band. Dined at Battn HQ. Danced in the tiny mess on a stone floor. Forrest was there and our string band.

November

Friday 1st
Sunny and warm. Went to Div. concert party.

Saturday 2nd
Made Acting Capt. Started to reconnoitre line which we were to attack in a day or two at 7.40 a.m. It was the same place that we had just come from. Got back at 12.30 p.m.

Sunday 3rd
Left at 5 p.m. Arrived at our half-way halt at Bellevue (a farm on the Wassigny–Ribeauville Road). Had supper there; Kelly and his staff came and finished off the whisky. Moved off at 11 p.m. Rain.

The Sambre Canal, 4th November 1918:
Ravenscroft's last attack.

Monday 4th

My Coy picked up life-belts at the Church at Rejet de Beaulieu as we were to cross the 2 reservoirs and canal if possible: failing that we were to cross at the lock. We had to carry enormously heavy patent collapsable boats through hedges etc. I didn't want them but had to have them. Zero 5.45 a.m. My orders were that if I couldn't cross at the Bosch footbridges within 20 minutes I was to go to the lock. When the 20 minutes were up the boats were still stuck in a hedge and the footbridges were down. I then collected the Coy and made for the lock. On the way I met D Coy coming to meet me saying that as they were held up at the lock they were coming to my crossing. I turned them back and we found a good many casualties at the lock. The Bosch had a lot of MGs in the remains of the upper storeys of a few houses. We finally got across and by that time we were all mixed up. My job was then to go along to the right with the Canal as my right flank to the 1st objective which was the main Landrecies–Oisy Road. (The bridge where it crossed the canal was of course blown up.) Collected about 20 men and proceeded along. Took several prisoners and ran some others to earth in the bank of the canal. Sneddon and Sladen (D Coy) joined me with a few men. Held up just short of the road by MG fire. Finally got there. Bosch didn't retaliate much with guns, afterwards Reserve Coy at Battn HG at Sans Fond on the same main road due E of L'Ermitage Farm. Fine day when the morning mist cleared. Bosch on the run and we ordered up cavalry. A very young, fat and inexperienced officer came up in charge but did nothing. Spent the night with HH Robinson in cubby hole by some abandoned Bosch guns. Oxley and Burrowes killed. Expected to be relieved but weren't.

[Findlay (Harrow) OC a Field Coy RE got VC for his work this day.]

Tuesday 5th
Misty and rainy day. Quiet – the Bosch had gone. Marched out (not relieved) at 4.30 p.m. Crossed the pontoon bridge (where some relieved civilians were struggling with a cart and horse) and marched through Pt Cambresis and Oisy to Wassigny. Rained hard. Slept in same billets as before.

[This attack was part of a great push[13], the last as a matter of fact. My morale was higher than it had ever been before; the casualties were comparatively light; altogether a most successful performance. It really suggested what the 1914 and previous war's fighting was like. No shell-holes to speak of and greeted by civilians on arrival at one's objective.] Forlong, my servant, was wounded, so I took Carpenter (Oxley's servant).

Wednesday 6th
Left Wassigny at 12.40 p.m. Raining hard all the time. Told we were really going out for a fortnight's well-earned rest. Marched through Andigny les Fermes, Regnicourt, Bohain, to Fresnoy le Grand. Arrived about 5 p.m. Not bad billets. Civilians very pleased to see us but very short of food. We gave them some. Cook came back.

Thursday 7th
Dull day. Dinkie to tea.

Friday 8th
Misty, rain all day. Went to Div. Concert Party with HH Robinson 5.30 p.m. in good Bosch theatre. Kiddle came back.

Saturday 9th
CO (Effie) and Dinkie to tea. Went to concert party. Lovely cloudless day. Walked over the downs in the morning. Dinkie to dinner and gave him chocolate blancmange made from not

very good eating chocolate from England. Heard about the Bosch coming to discuss terms.

Sunday 10th
Dinner at HQ mess. Played piano. Great excitement as to whether Bosch would sign. Church Parade in morning with all three padres (C of E, Non-Conformist, and RC) and Major-Gen. present.

Monday 11th
Took Coy out to make a range against a hillside. CO told me at 10.20 a.m. that Bosch had signed armistice. Told the Coy who cheered and threw their hats in the air. We then continued digging the range! Went to concert party in the evening. Dined with B, C and D Coys and went round to HQ Mess after and danced to the string band. There was a curious mixed feeling of joy and bewilderment.
   [I don't think we quite realised that we should never get orders to move up the line again for another push.]
   Dear old Rob[14] who had served throughout the whole war and had seen hundreds of us come and go nearly broke down. Had a quiet few minutes talk with Effie.

Tuesday 12th
Draft for A Coy of 38 arrived. Dined at Battn HQ. Babe Buckland, Standon and Beaumont arrived.

Wednesday 13th
Left 7.25 a.m. for buses to Favril (near Landrecies). Bosch had done an awful lot of damage as usual. Useless billets so had to do the billeting myself on arrival. D officers messed and slept with us. (Babe OC). Buses went through Bohain, Vaux Andigny, Catillon.

Thursday 14th
CO inspected draft. Orders for move failed to come in.

Friday 15th
Orders arrived 5.20 a.m. Left at 9.25 a.m. Marching through Grande Fayt, Marbain to Dompierre. Slept in house standing high on a rock. We had left the 'crocks' behind to go back to Details. They were to join us in Germany later, coming by train. All the crossroads were mined and occasionally they would go off. The REs did good work in removing the charges from a good many.

Saturday 16th
Orders arrived 1.30 a.m. Moved at 9 a.m. for Dimont but heard at last minute we were to go to Sars Poteries. Marched through St Aubin, Dourlers, Bois de Beugnies. Trouble with billets. Ended by A and D getting very comfortable one in a butcher's shop. Slept in sheets.

Sunday 17th
Church Parade 11.45 a.m. Talked with the liberated inhabitants. Humphrey to dinner. 3 men went on leave at midnight.

Monday 18th
Orders at 1.45 a.m. Left 7.58 a.m. for Thirimont via Solré le Château, Hestrud, Belgian Frontier, Grandrieu, Beaumont. Snowed a little. Discussed the War with two old women who gave me coffee and apples. Played piano in Humphrey's bedroom.

Tuesday 19th
Left 10.18 a.m. for Walcourt via Marzelle, Stree, Clermont, Castillon, Fontenelle, excellent billet with electric light etc. 2 brothers owned the house and regaled us with very good Madeira after dinner, also Burgundy.

Wednesday 20th
CO and Dinkie to dinner – more Burgundy; the brothers told us of the iniquity of the Bosch. Cleaned up a house which the Bosch had deliberately made filthy. Rabbit skins and broad beans months old in all the cupboards. Horses had been kept in the drawing room. Human excreta on the stairs and floors. This was only one house of many. Heard we were not to move next day owing to the difficulties of getting up rations owing to the roads and railways being blown up.

Thursday 21st
CO inspected the Coy at 14.00 hours. Lovely day. Gave my hosts rum punch after dinner. Now the war was over the 'spit and polish' campaign had begun in real earnest. Awful strife if a spot of mud was on clothes or equipment and this in spite of muddy weather and moving frequently. Even the cookers and limbers had to shine.

Friday 22nd
Lovely day. Went in the Church and saw the crutches of the miraculously cured cripples hanging on the walls. The tower had been blown up by the Bosch. Doc to dinner.

Saturday 23rd
Moved 9.16 a.m. to Morialme via Chastres, Fraire, Coy's turn to march behind 2nd line Transport to help it up frosty hills. Lovely day. Battn HQ in a racing man's house.

Sunday 24th
Moved at 9.30 to Falaen via Florennes and Flavion. Saw an effigy of the Kaiser dressed in Bosch uniform hung up in Flavion. Billeted in a Baronesses' château built in 1670. She had a husband and a very pretty daughter. Tea with the Baroness etc. Gracie to dinner. McCabe rejoined the Coy. Two pianos and 2 gramophones. First time ever billeted with even a passably pretty girl. Messed in the large dining room on our own.

Monday 25th
CO, Humphrey, Judd and Cook to dinner. Nearly all the other officers came in after. Our hosts came in, the Baron in shooting attire. Mlle danced very well. Gave her an English lesson after tea.

Tuesday 26th
Our hosts to tea. Gave them white bread! Astrop, Sneddon and Kiddle to dinner. Everyone came in after. Danced to the Band. Mlle danced every dance and drank everything we gave her without turning a hair – port, whisky and rum punch. The Baroness asked, sipping a strong whisky and soda, if English ladies drank this. Rob, in good form, he tackled the Baron in the best Rugger style. I gave and received English and French lessons after tea.

Wednesday 27th
Drizzle all day long. Heard we were not to move tomorrow. D'Argenton came back to D Coy. Babe and Maurice Sladen to dinner. Quieter evening but Mlle came in and danced. English lesson.

Thursday 28th
Battn ceremonial drill in morning. Band played after dinner. Kelly, Berkeley (Bde Major), Fergusson (Staff Capt.) and all the rest came in and danced. Lights went out so had candles. Ran short of drinks. English lesson.

Friday 29th
Took Mlle to watch Platoon football. Danced. Lights on and off. English lesson.

Saturday 30th
Took Suzanne to watch soccer match against No. 2 FA. We won
3–1. English lesson. Invited all three hosts to dinner. No bread
or coffee, otherwise quite a good dinner. Danced. Bunny Head
arrived back, but went to bed with possible appendicitis. Doc came
up to see him.

December

Sunday 1st
Bunny better. Left at 10 a.m. Suzanne took photos of the column
marching by. Went through Weillen, to Wespin Farm. The scenery
was very beautiful. Ravines, steep hills, fir trees and rocks. Went
for a walk after Office with Bunny. Lovely country. Charming
woman from whom we had roast chicken – one of the few left in
Belgium by the Bosch, and Madeira.

Monday 2nd
Moved at 10.20 through Dinant across the Meuse, Boisselles to Foy
Notre Dame. Arrived about 13.00. Cold mess and no stove. Welsh
(Sheerness) came over to see us from 1st Battn.

Tuesday 3rd
Looked over the Church built 1623 with a wonderful painted
ceiling. Moved at 8.30 through Celles to Ciergnon to a house of one
of King Albert's game-keepers. Wonderful scenery. One winding
hill from which we could see the head of the Bde about a mile in
front at the bottom. As Bunny remarked, one expected to see little
gnomes coming out of the pinnacled houses, as in Grimm's Fairy
Tales. Again no stove.

Wednesday 4th
Wet all day. Fed up. Tea at Battn HQ. Bunny, Humphrey, Mac
and Gracie went out boar hunting with the Keeper.

Thursday 5th
Fine day. Walked along a stream amongst fir trees. Tried to tune
piano in HQ Mess. Dined there.

Friday 6th
Lovely day. Went over King Albert's Château on the top of a rock.
Magnificent view. (2nd Bde HQ). Tea at Bde HQ. Saw the King's
bedroom, also the Queen's. Kelly slept in the former. A Coy played
B Coy at soccer. We lost 2–1.

Saturday 7th
Dull day. Went round to HQ after dinner. Draft of 11 arrived.

Sunday 8th
Took Mac over Château and grounds.

Monday 9th
Left at 9.14 for Haversin, through Bois de Mont Gautnier. Rained halfway through the march. Trouble in getting the Coy into billets. Amusing evening dosing the Landlady's daughter with rum and port. Battn HQ entertained magnificently by another Baron.

Tuesday 10th
Left at 9.19 for Melreux through Nettinne, Heure, Noiseaux, Devlin, Frouville. Arrived about 2.30 p.m. rather tired. Good billets for the men. Coy Mess like a seaside lodging house with Czerney's exercises being played next door on an out-of-tune piano.

Wednesday 11th
Moved at 10.00 to Erezee through Ny and Soy. More grand scenic effects. Arrived about 12.30 p.m. Rain in afternoon. Danced in HQ Mess (a hotel) to a good piano.

Thursday 12th
Rain. Played Bunny's clarinet and piccolo and my cornet. Collected all the tubs in the village so that the Coy could have a bath. Dined with D Coy and saw a photograph framed taken of a man after death and made to look as if he were alive.

Friday 13th
Rain all day. Dance and piano at HQ.

Saturday 14th
Moved at 9.10 a.m. to Odeigne. Marched through the clouds and Grandmenil and Manhay. Heavy going. Billeted in school with unpleasant schoolmaster.

Sunday 15th
Moved at 10.15 to Joubieval (Battn HQ at Ottre) through Belle Haie and Regne. Through the clouds again. 1900 feet above sea level.

Monday 16th
Moved in rain at 9.22 a.m. to Courtil through Salmchateau and Bovigny. Wore rain-coats. Good mess and bedroom. Orderly Room

160

in the Waiting Room of the Station (no trains, of course). Saw a motor car abandoned by the Bosch which LNL had collared.

Germany

Tuesday 17th
Moved at 8.10 a.m. for Krombach, through Behon, the frontier, where we marched past the Major-General standing by a fluttering Union Jack, and Maldingen. Rain and most awful mud. Civilians quite pleasant. We had to post sentries at all entrances to villages where we rested. No one was supposed to go out alone and all had to wear revolvers or swords (bayonets). No billet was to be left without someone to look after our kit. Transport had to have a guard. All this meant a great strain on our men as we were still fairly weak and were still moving nearly every day.

Wednesday 18th
Moved at 8.10 a.m. for Manderfeld. 17 miles through sleet and rain through St Vith, Schonberg, Andler. Billeted with curé who offered us apples but refused to drink a glass of wine that we offered out of politeness in return. We had strict orders to be polite but not to fraternise. Heard that I had got the MC. Dined at Battn HQ.

Thursday 19th
Moved at 9 a.m. to Dahlem through Hallschlag, Kronenburg, little snow, otherwise not unpleasant. Billeted on German Lieutenant who spoke English. Discussed the War with him also Germany and Ireland. He believed all the lies the Bosch government had told him (e.g. the French were the first to use gas).

Friday 20th
Tea with C Coy. Piano. Humphrey to dinner.

Saturday 21st
Moved at 10 a.m. to Blankenheim. Battn HQ in the Schloss. Coy mess in Hotel. Piano. Tea with Battn HQ. Danced after dinner at 2nd Bde HQ. Degenerate old man kept our hotel.

Sunday 22nd
Moved at 9.30 a.m. to Munstereifel through Tondorf, Holzmulheim, Eicherscheid. Quite a good-sized town. Heard after I left that the Frau and her daughter had slept on the floor of the dining room so that we officers should have the bedrooms. The mayor had ordered them to do it!

Monday 23rd
Moved at 9.23 to Palmersheim through Kirspenich and Flamersheim.
Rained in showers. Our mess had electric light put in 'while you
wait'.

Tuesday 24th
Great excitement as to whether our final billets would be good. Rob
had gone on a day or two before and had not sent very encouraging
notes. Moved at 9.22 to Glensgsdorf 4 kilos from Bonn, through
Miel, Buschhoven, Duisdorf. Quite good billets but Battn rather
scattered. A most interesting journey ended. On the whole all
civilians were very good to us. The Belgians all had triumphal
arches with messages of welcome. At some of the villages the
Mayors would turn out and make a speech to which the CO had
to reply as best he could.

Wednesday 25th
Quiet day.

Thursday 26th
Dinner at Battn HQ. CO and Dinkie appeared dressed up as fat
Bosch.

Friday 27th
Went to Bonn with Maurice, Doc and Gracie. Bought female
clothes. Took a cab back. Officer's Xmas dinner. Some of us in
fancy costume. Dancing. Maurice very negligé. Any state-owned
train was to carry up to 6 allies free.
[We all travelled free in state-owned trains and had compart-
ments reserved for us.] All uniformed officials were to salute
officers.

Saturday 28th
Men's Xmas dinner at midday. Sgts.' ditto in evening at which we
appeared afterwards. Went with Maurice to Bonn to take back
wigs.

Sunday 29th
Blackett, Royston, Young, Skinner and Finchon arrived after
spending weeks of misery with Details but without any com-
forts whatever at Vaux Andigny. Hinstridge (my CSM) went off
home as pivotal man (policeman). Judd got back. Indoor sports
in the morning.

Monday 30th
Moved at 11 a.m. for Alfter about 3 miles NW as we were in another Corp's area. Not such good officers' billets but the men's were a little better. The Battn was still rather scattered. Each Coy had a large hall for the men's billets. Blackett to dinner. My billet was in the Curé's house with a bathroom and electric light.

Tuesday 31st
Looked for Parade Ground but very difficult to find as everywhere was cultivation. Dinner at HQ. Blackett and Bunny also there. Drank in New Year with rum punch made by Judd.

1919

January

Wednesday 1st
Fine day. Discussed Pierrot Show. Tea and dinner with Blackett.

Thursday 2nd
Bicycled to Bonn with Blackett. Shopped. Lunch at Golden Stem. Cab home 6 p.m.

Friday 3rd
Dinner at Battn HQ. Rehearsal in theatre afterwards.

Saturday 4th
Soccer against Black Watch. 2 all. Maurice to dinner. Rehearsal.

Sunday 5th
Exam for some of the HQ Coy. This was to find out what men knew preparatory to dividing them into classes for education. The Doc was our Education Officer and we had filled up all sorts of forms during the march for the men. What courses they wanted to go on, what they wanted to be etc. Rehearsed after dinner.

Monday 6th
Pellett, White and Booth arrived with 100 odd men. Bunny went on PT Course at Cologne.

Tuesday 7th
Went by narrow-gauge train to Bonn with Blackett and Humphrey. Tea at Koenigshoff. Looked across the Rhine from the terrace. Back by cab.

Wednesday 8th
Bicycled with Blackett to Bonn. Lunch at Koenigshoff (pre-war name Grand Royal Hotel). Walked across the Rhine bridge to Beuel. Hired a piano and put it on a GS wagon. Mason and a draft arrived.

Thursday 9th
Coy route march.

HERE THE ORIGINAL DIARY CEASES

For the remainder of the time the mornings were spent in either education or drill; the idea being to bring up the standard of discipline to pre-war level and at the same time give the men a chance of using their brains while waiting to be demobilised.

In the afternoons there would be football or sports with an unlimited number of passes to Bonn.

We got together a few books and started a small library in the Recreation Room.

Our pierrot troupe afforded the performers endless amusement, but it was not quite what the men wanted. We tried to make it too artistic and didn't devote enough energy to the low comedy side. We toured the other Battns in the Bde, the Sussex giving us a good reception.

Arrangements were made later whereby parties of both officers and men could spend three days at hostels in Cologne. Blackett and I tried it. The great advantage was that we got plenty of good food (white bread etc.) and a variety of drinks at moderate prices.

We went several times to the opera which was excellent in every way. Good chorus, good orchestra and good scenery. Stalls were just under 8 marks!

About the middle of February, Blackett went to an Australian CCS at Enskirchen with 'flu and I followed 3 days later, a Div. Rest Camp at Rheinback being full. He then went off to No.14 General Hospital at Wimereux and I again followed. I was carried, feeling perfectly fit, on a stretcher into an ambulance train, crowds of Bosch gloating over me and no doubt saying 'One Englischer less in our Fatherland'. The train was not a real English-built ambulance train but an auxiliary one consisting of converted French trucks. There was a tiny piano on board which helped while away the time.

We left Enskirchen about 10 a.m. one morning, stayed hours on a Bonn siding and finally left Cologne at 10 p.m. When I woke next morning about 6 a.m. I looked out of the window and saw the ruins of Pont Fixe. I was actually travelling on the embankment that I had dug holes in at the beginning of August 1918 on the side of the La Bassée canal. Very annoyed that I had been asleep while going through La Bassée. Arrived at Wimereux about teatime.

Stayed over a week there and then had a fortnight's sick leave in England.

At the end of the leave I returned to Boulogne and travelled with Cook very comfortably in a converted real ambulance train now known as the 'Cologne – Boulogne Express'. We left Boulogne about 8 p.m. Stopped an hour at Charleroi (about 10 a.m.) where we had a shave and arrived at Cologne at 9 p.m.

We slept in a Bosch hotel and went on to Bonn next morning. There we found out that the Battn was at Dransdorf (next village to Alfter towards Bonn). We took a cab there and found them much reduced in strength.

The next day the Battn moved to Witterschliek where the Sussex had been. Our full band under Bmr Dunn had come out from England and played us on the march. My Coy was billeted at Heidgen about a kilometre away.

A day or two later, about the end of March, all officers and men who were not being demobilised and who were not Regulars left for the 9th London Reg. (TF) (QVR) at Duren. This was the real breaking up of the Battn and was a miserable day for both parties. Mac was in charge of the A Coy contingent. We all saw them off at the station and my old Coy cheered me (as all Coys did the CO) as the train steamed out.

A few days later Blackett, Cook, Mason and I left with the last batch of men, leaving only the Cadre behind. Forgetting all the horrors of the war I felt that this was the end of one of the happiest periods of my life. The Cadre came to see us off and waved fond farewells until the train bore us out of sight.

We arrived at Duren about noon and had tea with Mac and Gracie in their new home. Saw some of the old faces in the streets and the mess waiters waited on us. This cheered us up a little.

Next day we travelled in a truck with our valises (quite comfortable) leaving Duren about 11 a.m. We crossed the front line at Armentières the next day about 4 p.m. and arrived at St Pol near Dunkerque about 10 p.m. As we passed near various places where we had been during the war so various incidents and people passed through our thoughts.

During the journey the train stopped at places where we received free meals. Some energetic persons even washed, and Mason had to run a considerable distance after the train with braces and towel flying in the wind.

We stayed in a hut camp in the Dunes at St Pol for two or three days on the site of our Battn tent camp in July 1917.

Blackett and I tried to get up to Nieuport, but it couldn't be done without great expense.

We crossed from Dunkerque to Dover and the train took us straight to the Crystal Palace where we were disembodied or demobilised (I never could find out which) at 10 p.m. on April 11th 1919. We parted at Victoria as civilians each to go to his own home; but that feeling of elation one experienced on arriving in London on leave was conspicuously absent.

References

[1] *See* Monday 13th August 1917.
[2] First Aid Nursing Yeomanry.
[3] A total of 48 officers of the rank of Brig.-General and above were killed in the Great War (*Officers Died in the Great War*, HMSO, 1919).
[4] This German offensive was code-named MICHAEL but is normally referred to as the Kaiser's Battle.
[5] Doc Ward had been captured, along with 'Strafer' Gott and 8 other officers on 10th July 1917 near Nieuport Bains.
[6] i.e. Robinson.
[7] This was the 2nd phase of the great German offensive that began on 21st March, this time further north. It was code-named GEORGETTE.
[8] i.e. Operations and Training.
[9] The epidemic of Spanish Influenza caused about 27 million deaths nationwide between 1918 and 1920, considerably more than the total deaths suffered by all belligerents in the War.
[10] Field Ambulance.
[11] It was the considered view of one MO that 'Had it not been for the rum ration I do not think we should have won the war'. (Richard Holmes, *The Firing Line*, 1985).
[12] Ravenscroft wrote to his mother on the 26th 'A small piece of shell has had the impudence to hit me in the chin. Thank the Lord it didn't hit my teeth. It is not serious, not even going through to my mouth, and I do not expect to be away long . . .'
[13] In fact both 3rd and 4th Armies took part in the battle on the Sambre. Altogether 4 VCs were won on this day. In Germany revolution broke out.
[14] *See* note 19th November, 1915.